"Ambassador Buallay's fine book appears at a very opportune moment of history. At a time when war in Ukraine has posed a fundamental challenge to the post-World War II order and the pandemic has exposed the short-comings of existing mechanisms of international cooperation, it is more important than ever before to insist—as he does—on the vital and irreplaceable role of the United Nations and its related institutions. That they are imperfect is an argument for reform not for disregarding them. Ambassador Buallay brings the experience of a lifetime in diplomacy to the vital question of how international life is to be better organized for the benefit of all. His real theme is no less than mankind's future. This book should be read by all who aspire to leadership."

—Ambassador Bilahari Kausikan

Former Permanent Representative of Singapore to the United Nations and former Director of the Middle East Institute in Singapore

"It is always worth listening to the voices of elected members of the UN Security Council. Jassim Buallay's book gives a Bahraini perspective on its workings, and it makes sobering reading for the privileged Permanent Members. In a world where soft power has an increasingly greater impact, the P5 should be calculating how much they may be losing from the way they attempt to further their own interests in this body. His plea for a more urgent approach to reform should be heard while the UN still retains some relevance for international peace."

—Ambassador Sir Jeremy Greenstock

Former Permanent Representative of the United Kingdom to the United Nations

The United Nations in the Balance

Challenges to Effective Crisis Response

Jassim Buallay

Fairleigh Dickinson

Vancouver · Madison · Teaneck · Wroxton

PUBLISHED BY FAIRLEIGH DICKINSON UNIVERSITY PRESS
Copublished by BLOOMSBURY ACADEMIC
Bloomsbury Publishing Inc, 1359 Broadway, 12th Floor, New York, NY 10018, USA
Bloomsbury Publishing Plc, 50 Bedford Square, London, WC1B 3DP, UK
Bloomsbury Publishing Ireland, 29 Earlsfort Terrace, Dublin 2, D02 AY28, Ireland

BLOOMSBURY, BLOOMSBURY ACADEMIC and the Diana logo are trademarks of Bloomsbury Publishing Plc

First published in the United States of America 2026

Fairleigh Dickinson University Press gratefully acknowledges the support received for scholarly publishing from the Friends of FDU Press.

ISBN: HB: 978-1-68393-387-8
ePDF: 978-1-68393-713-5
eBook: 978-1-68393-618-3

Typeset by Integra Software Services Pvt. Ltd.

For product safety-related questions, contact productsafety@bloomsbury.com.

To find out more about our authors and books visit www.bloomsbury.com and sign up for our newsletters.

Contents

Foreword

Over the past half millennium, humanity has progressed from the printing press and the slide rule to the internet and artificial intelligence. It has witnessed a limited transnational trade in textiles, spices, and slaves develop into a global marketplace in which multinational conglomerates endeavor to sell all things to all people. A world with meaningful, albeit vacillating and hotly contested, national borders has become one in which ecological, economic, health, and security problems know no borders.

Foremost among the problems facing the world today are conflicts between countries and conflicts involving non-state actors. These conflicts are no longer local events threatening the lives and livelihoods of people in particular corners of the globe. Rather, these conflicts have widespread effects on international markets, on the spread of contagious diseases, and on the migration of refugees; they also provide fertile soil for all manner of international criminal activity. When we consider that there are more than one hundred active armed conflicts in the world today, the overall scale and cost (in human and economic terms) is simply staggering.

The United Nations was created in the wake of the Second World War to curtail such conflicts. Although it was established in the middle of the twentieth century, the UN has its intellectual and ethical roots in the Enlightenment, when ideas of universal rights, rule of law, the free market, and constitutional government, as well as a cosmopolitan mindset, flourished in universities and *salons*.

Since the Enlightenment, we have seen the emergence and codification of universal principles of individual rights in the constitutions of many countries, although these principles are inconsistently realized in most. They have also been infused in international law, including the Universal Declaration of Human Rights and other international conventions. These Enlightenment principles include but are not limited to: (1) Rights to life, liberty, and security of persons; (2) Rights of due process and equal recognition, as well as freedom from discrimination; (3) Freedom of thought, conscience, religion, and expression, including the right to engage in public reasoning; (4) Freedom of association and assembly and the right to universal suffrage; and (5) Rights to property, a decent standard of living, health, and education.

Some Enlightenment philosophers even envisioned a world confederation of semi-autonomous republics that would come together for the sole purpose of preventing war and its ill-omened consequences. Among the Enlightenment thinkers, the Prussian philosopher Immanuel Kant offered one of the most powerful and enduring visions of a confederation of free states—a civil union of civil unions—in a long essay titled *Perpetual Peace: A Philosophical Essay*. Kant specifies that this confederation would not be a unified state, i.e., "a world-republic," and would not require a unified government.[1] On the contrary, each member state would be sovereign and self-governing with respect to internal affairs, with these prerogatives defended by the strength of the entire confederation according to previously agreed-upon international laws. Such a confederation would consist of all nations that incorporate principles of freedom and equality in their internal constitutions. In other words, despotic states need not apply, although constitutional monarchies embodying these principles would be welcome.

In this context, the charter of the United Nations would appear to be a quintessential Enlightenment document and perhaps even the basis for the perpetual peace envisioned by Kant. However, it falls short when it comes to the principle of equality between sovereign states. Specifically, the charter contradicts Enlightenment principles in the section detailing the powers of the Security Council and, most importantly, the prerogatives of its five permanent members. These exceptional powers include the authority to veto any council resolution, even when the council is otherwise unanimous. The veto power has time and time again prevented the UN from taking action to forestall or foreshorten military conflicts around the world.

The Permanent Five also have the power to veto any proposed amendment to the charter itself. Consequently, only the Permanent Five themselves, acting in unison, could amend the charter to eliminate (or curtail) their own exceptional powers. Although granting these exceptional powers to the Permanent Five was a condition for the charter's passage, today these powers create paralysis and distrust of the United Nations as a whole.

It has often been said by modern champions of globalism that if the United Nations did not exist, it would need to be invented. Such pronouncements cannot be the end of our conversations about the UN. Rather, they can only be fruitful when, in the spirit of the Enlightenment, they set the table for critiques by the loyal opposition.

The book is a call to action for the UN's loyal opposition. Its author, a career diplomat and international civil servant, is passionately committed to the idea of the United Nations and its many positive contributions to peace and prosperity around the world. However, he is acutely aware of its many shortcomings. His analysis of these shortcomings addresses the challenges posed by the prerogatives of the Permanent Five but also identifies numerous other ways that UN crisis response and social development outcomes can be improved through institutional reform.

It is addressed less to academic specialists than it is to citizens of the world who need to understand how the United Nations works, what it has achieved, what it can achieve, where it falls short, and what must be done to fulfill its potential—an idealistic premise. It is, for all that, addressed to me, and I hope, sincerely, also to you.

Jason A. Scorza (1968–2024)
Vice Provost for International Affairs
Fairleigh Dickinson University
December 20, 2023

Note

1 Emmanuel Kant, *Perpetual Peace: A Philosophical Essay*. Translated by Campbell Smith. London: Swan Sonnenschein, 1903 [1795], 69.

Preamble

In the jargon of the United Nations Security Council, "preamble" refers to the beginning paragraph of a draft resolution in which the basic details of the subject matter are mentioned. This preamble is followed by the working paragraphs that reflect the decisions of the council relating to the subject. These working paragraphs are binding in their application by all member states, while the preamble is not.

The United Nations System, or simply the System, is a complex conglomeration of interrelated organizations. Each of the six main organs of the System has several subsidiary bodies, programs, and funds that may or may not be administered separately. Harboring any pretension of knowing everything and anything about the System is almost impossible, if not unattainable. This being said, one cannot be silent about the unsatisfactory state of affairs that the United Nations Organization finds itself in, and one cannot afford not to dig in and unearth some or all of the causes that have made the organization arrive at the present unfavorable situation.

This book draws on my experience with the United Nations System, both from within and without, in the sense of having worked in the System as an international civil servant and later as Bahrain's diplomatic representative to the United Nations. My first experience with the United Nations was in one of the specialized agencies, the United Nations Educational, Scientific and Cultural Organization (UNESCO), in Paris in the seventies, and the second was as a representative to the United Nations at its headquarters in New York City in the nineties. While I spent over thirty years working at and with the United Nations, this service is neither inclusive nor conclusive, for the simple reason that the System is so intricate, complicated, and huge that it has outgrown and overstretched itself over three-quarters of a century.

This book tries to point out the disadvantages of inflated size, budgets, personnel, the number and location of headquarters, as well as—above all—mandates of the System. It does so as a first attempt to point out the problems from the standpoint that we need to know these elements well enough before we can think about solutions to solve the problems they present. Emphasizing the shortcomings of the System may seem futile, based on the erroneous view that the United Nations System is simply too big and complicated to allow any productive reforms to be attempted, much less achieved. Rather than finding solutions to redress unsatisfactory outcomes, such outcomes are accepted as the consequence of the System's size and complexity. Failure ceases to be an occasional worry and instead becomes the norm, a routine rather than exceptional situation.

This seemingly hopeless and desperate conclusion has lodged itself in the minds of those who work for the System, a situation that unintentionally contributes to its size and complexities. By contrast, the resulting routine is encouraged intentionally by those influential member states, especially the veto holders, who prioritize their national interests in the work of the United Nations over the interests of the organization. Representatives of member states represent nationalism, while the United Nations as an organization symbolizes multilateralism. However, you do not often hear the word "multilateralism" in world media or in the affairs of United Nations member states, as nationalistic interests have submerged it even when the work deals with the United Nations System.

The problems that beset the System, which are the concern of this book, can be illustrated by a few examples taken from my experience. The UNESCO headquarters is situated in the beautiful Fontenoy Square in the chic Seventh Arrondissement of Paris where around 2,200 staff members work at the headquarters and its field offices. In the corridor that lies beyond the entrance, the visitor will see a bank branch, a post office, a cafeteria, a restaurant, and other facilities that are provided for the benefit of those who try hard to advance education, science, and culture in the member states of an organization that was born at the same time that the United Nations was established in 1945. As if catering to these three major mandates is not enough, UNESCO has added more focus areas, such as communication and maintenance of historical sites—

though they will tell you it is part of culture—and things like technology. All these are big and important undertakings in their own right. Naturally, this is a costly affair both in budget and staff. While this expansion might be logical in terms of UNESCO's terms of reference, it has created an environment filled with complications and overlaps. Above all, it allowed routine to settle in when it comes to executing the programs. Routine is an enemy of creativity. For example, instead of making sure mandate tasks are done thoroughly, the worry became getting the job done quickly before the biennium is over so that they can present the General Conference with a fresh budget estimate for approval. Delegations to the General Conference are usually headed by ministers of education or their participating deputies, and deliberations over budget approvals can involve some heated exchanges, especially when they concern developing countries in Africa, Asia, and Latin America, or members from the Pacific Islands, since the developmental projects in those countries fall under the auspices of UNESCO. Hence, you will find ministers of these countries going to great lengths to encourage the Conference to approve the biennial budget, so much so that one minister from a developing country got so carried away by emotion that he had a heart attack. There the man lay on the podium while one delegate after another continued to urge the Conference to approve the budget, all wishing the minister well at the beginning of their speeches. The draft program and budget were unanimously approved.

The UNESCO Secretariat, headed by the director-general, has feeble accountability, and control is centralized in the Parisian headquarters. In my time there, the majority of staff, including the director-general, were French with this head being a veteran professional who climbed the ladder to the top. This, while the development challenges they were meant to address are found elsewhere. The situation at the time was eased by establishing a field office and appointing a non-French director-general, but the disconnect between the administration and the communities it is intended to serve remains because of the ever-expanding size of the organization and the scope of its mandates.

UNICEF, the other organization I worked for, is a different case, as it cares for children before, during, and after birth. Since many UNICEF employees have children, the work of the Fund is made easy by all concerned, including the delegates and representatives of its member states. UNICEF's popularity and the approval of its work can be seen in the source of its budget. Unlike other United Nations Organizations that rely on obligatory financial contributions from member states, UNICEF gets its money from voluntary contributions to do its work, and, because UNICEF is very popular there, most of it comes from the biggest contributor to the United Nations, the United States of America. That's why, traditionally, an American occupies the post of the executive director. To demonstrate the almost unanimity of the Fund work, and the contrast with the battles for budgets at UNESCO, when I chaired the Admin and Finance Committee, we had little difficulty convincing delegates to approve the funds necessary to build a full-fledged headquarters suitable for productive working conditions to replace the rented floors in an all-purpose building. The negotiations did not require the usual East and West stalling and give-and-take arguments at UNESCO. The only worrying thing that comes to mind is that with the worsening economic conditions in some parts of the world, there will be a decreasing effect on the voluntary contributions that UNICEF receives.

My third experience with the multilateral system was as a permanent representative to the organization. In this capacity, I, together with the members of my delegation, campaigned successfully for Bahrain to gain a seat on the International Security Council of the United Nations for a two-year period, and as the head of the delegation, I served as president of the council for the customary one-month period. Immediately after the termination of that two-year term on the Security Council, my delegation and I campaigned, again successfully, for Bahrain to obtain the membership of the Economic and Social Council (ECOSOC) for the prescribed period of three years, during which I was chairman of the Council's Humanitarian Commission. The combination of the two memberships gave Bahrain and its permanent delegation a comprehensive experience in the political, economic, and social affairs as well as the admin work of the Secretariat by virtue of being physically present in New York City. On the judicial side, Bahrain assumed membership of the International Law Commission for three successive terms.

The discussions in this book are rooted in the experience gained from the United Nations System, as is the analysis of the urgent and timely reforms that are called for. The call for these reforms emanates from a firm conviction about the immense advantages of the United Nations mandates and a belief in the work the UN does. The book tries to point out that the reforms are long overdue, so much so and in so many areas that there is a danger of overlooking them for the benefit of the routine day-to-day work.

Reforming the United Nations System is essential because continuing to lean on the routine work to do the job will hasten the demise of the influence that the organization can exert in world affairs, especially since it is the only organization mandated to take care of such affairs. Reforming the System is not only possible but probable if its member states, especially the influential ones and particularly the veto holders, show a genuine intention to undertake the necessary changes. This they can do if, first and foremost, they believe in and treat the United Nations as a distinct international organization (United Nations Culture) with its own methods of work. At the moment, they treat United Nations affairs, which are multilateral, in a way similar to the way they treat their own governments, which is rooted in nationalism, just because they are the ones who finance the United Nations. The second fundamental condition for genuine reform is that member states should not prioritize their own national interests and muddle them with those of the United Nations affairs. If the veto holders adopt this healthy approach, even the veto that so far has been so employed to serve national interests when it should be used for international interests could be ameliorated. If the veto is used to serve international interests, it could be cast in a positive manner against any member state that means harm to the mandates of the United Nations and the execution of these goals.

This book does not claim to have all the answers nor suggest all the required approaches for serious, productive reforms necessary to make the United Nations System more adaptive to a changing world. The book can claim, however, that it has provoked some important discussion pertaining to the long-overdue reforms. If those issues that emanate in part from a personal experience but also from other sources are treated seriously, we might see light at the end of the seventy-five-year-old tunnel.

Thus ends the preamble, with no binding application. It is followed by the working paragraphs—just like the General Assembly but unlike the Security Council.

1

Establishing the System of the United Nations

The United Nations System was created in 1945 in the aftermath of the Second World War because its predecessor, the League of Nations—itself created after the First World War—failed to prevent the second war. The second time around, the winning camp wanted to make sure that things could not get out of hand in managing world affairs again, so they gave themselves what they called a "veto power," which is the right of a firm negation of anything they do not approve of. A parallel second privilege that they also bestowed on themselves was permanent membership in the United Nations Security Council, as opposed to a temporary period of two years for the other members of the council. The resolutions of the Security Council are binding for all members of the organization to observe and apply.

In this setting, a system was established to take care of all global affairs—political, economic, social, judicial, and anything related to them. The terms of reference and mandate of the United Nations System are international to the extent that if the system were not there, it ought to have been created, or else the world would have been left to be torn by wars yet again. However, the mandate was so huge and so varied that the task of making it work was colossal. It can be categorized into two main responses by the UN System in managing world affairs.

First, there is the development side, in which the organization expertise is geared toward assisting its member states in all developmental problems that they face, be they monetary, educational, environmental, health, agricultural, or industrial. The development side also includes relief services. This is a routine, straightforward endeavor. The projects relating to these aspects are undertaken by the specialized agencies which are under the auspices of the ECOSOC, an important development organ of the United Nations. The second side, the monetary side, of the mandate is controlled by the Bretton Woods Institutions. All these developmental projects give the United Nations System a marked positive response owing to the immense and important job that renders clear and far-reaching results.

The political issues that are handled by the United Nations fall within the responsibilities of the Security Council and the General Assembly. These issues are discussed, and relevant resolutions concerning them are taken. The response of the United Nations in this case is somewhat compromised. While some degree of success has been achieved on some issues, like preventing the secession of the Katanga and South Kasai regions from the Democratic Republic of Congo (DRC), unsatisfactory outcomes have been detected for others.[1] The reasons for this come both from within and outside the power of the United Nations System. It might be that the United Nations did not move quickly, or the response was beyond its capacity logistically, or that the mandate given to it by its member states kept changing or shifting with time and events. One should not exclude here the conflict between the national and international interests of member states. Finally, the veto power of those who hold it should not be discounted when it comes to decision-making.

The United Nations System needs a comprehensive reform so that its handling of international issues will be more effective, both for the routine response and especially for the crisis response. This reform should be based on knowledge gained from past experience but also take into consideration the future evolving and changing world that gave the United Nations a more comfortable working atmosphere in the midst of the rivalry between Western and Eastern camps during the Cold War and a more difficult one in its aftermath. This reform will also save the System from a relative loss of effectiveness when it comes to dealing with international issues, the very mandate given to it by its member states.

In 1945, after months of negotiations and the death of its champion, President Franklin D. Roosevelt, the United Nations Charter was unanimously approved in San Francisco, on the west side of the United States of America and facing the then undeveloped Asian countries far from the decision-making centers in the United States and Europe, the battlefield of two major world wars, where peace was intended to be spread instead of war. Subsequent to the signing of the charter, the first meetings of the UN General Assembly and UN Security Council were convened in London on January 16, 1946, and January 17, 1946, respectively.

Why then should the seat of the UN be in the United States and not in Europe? The answer, simply, is that the United States emerged from the Second World War as the biggest, richest, and most powerful country in the West. Having helped Europe win the war against the Germans and their allies, principally Italy and Japan, the United States subsequently financed the continent's redevelopment. Therefore, with time, decision-makers at the UN saw it as more logical and beneficial to locate the headquarters on the east side of the United States, facing Europe, and particularly in New York City, the business hub of the United States. The city did not offer its best prime land to the international organization but offered it a location near a river harbor that housed an electricity-generating station and a slaughterhouse and that saw barges crossing the East River carrying all kinds of merchandise. Construction of the UN headquarters began in 1948, and the building was officially opened in 1951. In the meantime, the organization was housed in temporary accommodations, initially at Hunter College, part of the City University of New York (from March to June 1946), and then in Lake Success, NY, in a disused facility of the Sperry Gyroscope Company, a major defense contractor during the Second World War.

Today, the midtown side of the East River area where the UN headquarters is located is considered one of the chic areas of Manhattan, housing sumptuous apartments and hotels—thanks to its personnel and member states' diplomats, among other things. In fact, the US permanent representative resides permanently in a suite at the famous Waldorf-Astoria Hotel. A pertinent question in this context is: Should a big organization be housed in a big, powerful country?

The structure of the UN System established in the Big Apple grew gradually in size, budget, and cost to the membership. The organization needed a vast number of personnel to sustain this growth and to oversee the reconstruction and development of the damage caused by the two devastating world wars; as a consequence, the UN System began to satisfy that need, which in turn justified further expansion of the System to maintain the varied and comprehensive mandate of the UN. The recovery and developmental projects in the aftermath of the Second World War did not leave room for controversy, and the UN's response to their realization was satisfactory because those projects were economic and social in nature. After all, there is no development without peace, just as there is no peace without development. However, the challenge to the efficiency of the System in carrying out the economic and social part of the mandate became more felt when the System expanded in size, complexity, budget, and staff, and when coordination and coherence began to suffer.

Despite its growth, the UN continued to cooperate in a satisfactory manner with its members on developmental and social needs projects. It is only when peacekeeping crises have arisen that the UN System has been put to the test, especially in those conflicts that endure for a long time despite engaging the required men and material to make peace. In 1996, the UN had forty-one unique peace missions scattered around the world. Most of these missions are still in the field, where trouble spots have been or are still active. There are several reasons for this, but these crises have shown that the shortcomings of the UN System regarding crisis management are there and real. As a result, the need for a far-reaching reform of the System is more than called for if we want the UN to be willing and able to play the role stipulated by its mandates in a satisfactory way.

The growth of the United Nations, with all the negative outcomes that come with it by way of overlapping and repetition and the loss of money and time, is so intricate that an outgoing official has commented that, "If you locked a team of evil geniuses in a laboratory, they could not design a bureaucracy so maddeningly complex."[2] Imagine, therefore, the enormity of the task of reforming such a system, though it is a must. If we do not reform the UN, it will be difficult to put up with a system that has not adapted itself to a changing world for so long. On the development side, and to a lesser extent compared to peacekeeping, natural disasters have created the need for relief at the expense of developmental projects.

In the strict sense of the word, genuine reforms have not been undertaken. Otherwise, the picture would have changed the face of the United Nations System to a brighter one. Rather, piecemeal changes have been introduced that do not satisfy the desired goal of revitalizing a complex machine that has fallen into disrepair to such an extent that it is unable to satisfy its peacekeeping and developmental mandates. Witness the calamities of earthquakes, floods, and brushfires that are presently occurring almost at the same time.

The United Nations Organization cannot be held entirely responsible for its below-expectation performance. It might be held responsible for its complicated spider web of an administration that tries to handle too many things, and that affects its performance in a negative way. However, the main cause of the UN's failings is the control its member states have over its operations, especially its influential members. In essence, the rivalry among veto holders leads them to put their national interests ahead of international interests. This has nothing to do with the multilateralism represented by the United Nations System. These influential member state governments hesitate to open up participation in United Nations affairs to non-governmental institutions such as businesses, NGOs, trade unions, and city and regional administrations for their participation, moves that will improve global governance according to the thinking of the present secretary-general, António Guterres.

Has the United Nations System situation reached the point of a crisis? When an organization fails to pass messages about its work to governments and citizens of its member states, when its governing bodies pass decisions that are not respected nor applied by those states despite this being obligatory according to the organization's charter, and when those decisions are vetoed by some members in one of its most important organs, one cannot help but feel that there is a problem, and a major one at that. What makes the situation desperate is that running the United Nations System is a costly affair that drains the financial resources of some needy member states. Those resources could alternatively be used in indispensable economic and social projects. It is not in the interest of all United Nations member states to finance the work of the organization and then put sticks in its wheels of operations.

What to do to make the working atmosphere of the United Nations System healthier? The answer is to do our utmost, urgently. Reforming the United Nations has been delayed for a long time, to the extent that its present performance has led to a *de facto* conviction that it is beyond repair. Discouraging as this is, we cannot allow this belief to override the necessity of reforming the System. It is beyond time to do something for the United Nations so that confidence in its work can be restored. The modalities for reform are many and widespread, but unless the intent to undertake such change is there, chances are that the complexities of the system will make a fertile terrain for a merry-go-round of actions that will fall short of real reform, causing a waste of time and resources, which becomes in itself the target instead of the ways and means of realization.

Major wars, with all that accompanies them by way of casualties, human suffering, and material damage, not to mention civilian displacement, are not new to the world that we are living in. However, with the evolution of human lifestyles that resulted from the industrial revolution, and with it the sophistication of armaments made, major wars became catastrophic—the antagonists involved would not accept any truce; they simply rearmed and started again. Several attempts were made to find peace after these wars, but to no avail. This became abundantly clear after the devastating First World War. In the end, weary of fighting, belligerents began to buy into the idea of some sort of long-term peace, but since they were party to the conflicts, they could not also be party to peace. Some sort of common peace was necessary to end that war, i.e., a kind of multilateralism was needed, an international body that had no interest in any warring factions. This kind of thinking was a first in politics, considering that until then the national interests of states were the prime mover of their policies, both in war and in peace. In fact, it was the first attempt ever to try a common collective effort to put an end to major wars. And so an organization with a world character was born. It went by the name of the League of Nations.

Serious discussion of forming an international organization had been ongoing since the outbreak of the First World War in 1914, but it was only after US President Woodrow Wilson presented his Fourteen Points document in January 1918 that work officially began toward making such an organization a reality. The League of Nations was officially established on January 10, 1920, at the Paris Peace Conference (January 1919 to August 1920), with a membership of forty-eight nations. Its headquarters were initially located in London, UK, before moving to Geneva, Switzerland. The core mission of the League of Nations was finding solutions to conflicts before they developed into major wars, as had happened in the First World War. In other words, to treat the developing conflicts peacefully before the parties involved resort to arms. President Wilson was unable to convince the American Congress to join the League of Nations, but his points of peace did form the basis for the League of Nations.

Soon after its formation, the League of Nations started mediating to solve several border and territory disputes, proceeding cautiously in order not to undermine its authority, especially since it was the first time in modern history that such work was being undertaken. The organization did have some success, notably in the General Treaty for Renunciation of War as an Instrument of National Policy of 1928, commonly known as the Kellogg-Briand Pact, which related to the *raison d'être* of the League as an organization established to advocate peace by preventing war. By 1934, sixty-three nations had signed onto the Treaty. However, when it was put into practice, it could not hold, as is witnessed by the 1931 invasion of Mongolia by Japan, one of the original signatories. The World Disarmament Conference, held between 1932 and 1934, did not ultimately secure the reduction of armaments as laid out in Article 8 of the League's charter, but it did show that nations were willing to work together toward such a goal. Another achievement was scored by the establishment of the Minorities Commission which aimed to protect minorities. It was an important first step in the protection of human rights.

While the League of Nations had some notable achievements on the road to peace, these achievements generally involved disputes that were small and limited, and it seems that the remnants of the First World War were not entirely buried, as shown by the appearance of figures like Benito Mussolini and Adolf Hitler, who saw the League as an Allied Organization, and the outbreak of the Second World War in 1939, which the League neither had the means nor the mandate to prevent. In 1943, at the Teheran Conference, the Allied Camp agreed that a different body should replace the League: that organization became the United Nations. By thinking of having a replacement for the League, rather than abandoning the idea, the countries of the World manifested again the desperate desire for an enduring peace because the world had suffered enough human casualties and material damage because of devastating wars.

The reason for establishing an alternative international organization was obvious: the League of Nations had failed to prevent another major war. In retrospect, it does seem that ending the First World War was only a temporary break to rearm and start another major war with more sophisticated weapons and different actors.

The UN Charter, adopted on June 25, 1945, came into effect on October 24 of that year, marking the establishment of a replacement for the League of Nations. Once again an American, in the person of President Franklin Roosevelt, with the help of the British prime minister, Winston Churchill, played a major role in making the organization become a reality. The two men, tired of the war that had ravaged Europe, vowed to create an organization for the promotion of peace, so the United Nations was formed on June 26, 1945, at the UN Conference on International Organization in San Francisco. Why in the United States? Simply because Europe had been severely damaged by the war and Europeans were neither mentally nor materially prepared and willing to engage in the creation of a sizable international organization such as the UN. Fifty-one states joined at the formation of the organization, with the failure of the League of Nations fresh in their minds; the number of member states has since swelled to 193 member states, with two observer states.

The first General Assembly of the United Nations was held in London. At that meeting, it was decided that the permanent headquarters would be in the United States. As Charlene Mires mentions in her book *Capital of the World: The Race to Host the United Nations*, "Americans in more than two hundred cities and towns seized upon this transitional moment in history to suggest—quite seriously—that their own hometowns or regions would be the best possible choice as the future Capital of the World."[3] This marks a complete change of heart on the part of America and the Americans when we note that President Wilson failed to ignite American interest in the League of Nations. In the end, New York City was strongly favored by everybody, including the first secretary-general, the Norwegian Trygve Lie. The temporary locations in the Sperry Gyroscope Factory and the Hunter College gym in the Bronx were clearly unsuitable for an organization of this scope and stature. So, with a lot of hard work and determination on the part of the Rockefeller brothers, including Nelson, who served as the US secretary of state and was a supporter of the UN, they secured a location in Turtle Bay on the East End of Manhattan Island. It was not a prime location, as the area housed slaughterhouses, tenement buildings, and a power station. In addition, there were barges transporting all kinds of merchandise. Today, thanks in part to the UN presence there, the area is one of the prime locations in New York City.

Despite the initial decision to locate the headquarters in New York, it is worth asking whether an international organization should be housed in an influential big member state. It is noteworthy that most of the UN specialized agencies are located in small, neutral Switzerland. It makes sense to have the UN financial institutions at the Bretton Woods Institutions based in Washington, as the United States is a leader in free economies, as well as a major contributor to the UN budget. However, relations between international organizations such as the UN and big influential states in the world have not always been rosy.

When they created the UN, the victorious Allied countries who defeated the Axis Camp wanted to make sure that devastating wars like the First and Second World Wars do not happen ever again, so they gave themselves an additional two privileges in addition to being members of the most powerful organ in the UN System, the Security Council. These additional privileges were permanent membership of the council and the right to veto any resolution which is not to their liking and approval. Since the five are self-appointed and permanent, they are obviously not elected. Together, they comprise a third of the fifteen-member Security Council, with the remaining ten members being elected for a tenure of two years by the General Assembly. Candidates for membership must come from the five geographical groups of the UN (Asia, Africa, Latin America, Western, and Eastern groups).

The Security Council is the only organ in the UN System whose resolutions are binding for all the members. It is true that no major war has happened in the world since the formation of the UN, though the world is at present dotted with local and regional wars, directly or by proxy. However, the council membership of five permanent members with the power of veto and ten non-permanent is neither democratic nor fair (15 from a total of 193 members). What's more, it induces the council members—especially the permanent ones—to prioritize their national interests vis-à-vis the UN's international goals. This abnormal situation does not allow the organization to work in a healthy atmosphere to effectively realize its goals relating to multilateralism.

Commemorating the seventy-fifth anniversary of the organization, *The Economist* published a ten-page Special Report on the UN in June 2020. Citing the organization's reaction to the COVID-19 pandemic, the authors of the Special Report have this to say, "A divided UN Security Council has been missing in action" and "the UN Security Council has confirmed its dysfunctionality."[4] This is a vivid example of the failure of the System to deal with an urgent global problem. It is partly due to the imbalance in the council's membership and the rivalry among the veto holders. Despite this major hurdle, the UN has succeeded relatively well in achieving economic and social development in its member states—though that achievement is hampered when it comes to its peacekeeping mission, partly because of the existence of the veto power that lies in the hands of the permanent five members of the Security Council.

The Charter

The charter of the United Nations was signed on June 26, 1945, in San Francisco at the conclusion of the United Nations Conference on International Organization and came into force on October 24, 1945.

It is significant to note that the charter's brief introduction starts with "We the peoples of the United Nations" and not the governments because the reality is that nothing can be done these days for any people without the approval of their governments. It is also worth noting that the word "determined" was printed as part of the lead-in to the opening statement of the charter to emphasize the willingness to prevent wars and make peace, making the "human person" the center of this exercise, confirming their right to a peaceful coexistence and to an economic and social development following the establishment of that peace. As to the Purposes and Principles found in Chapter One of the charter, they are noble ideals, but with time they have given way to the hard realities that stand as obstacles in the road to their application. This is due mainly to the decisions of some world governments to prioritize their national interests vis-à-vis the international cooperation called for by the UN System; we should not discount in this regard, yet again, the self-acquired veto that the Permanent

Five hold in the UN Security Council. As long as the UN member states follow a policy of rivalry and confrontation rather than cooperation, there is bound to be a contradiction between national and international interests.

Furthermore, there are some observations that need to be made regarding certain articles in the charter. Principle 1 in Article 2 states that "the Organization is based on the principle of the sovereign equality of all its Members," implying that this charter cannot authorize the UN to intervene in the jurisdiction of any member state. Yet at the same time, Principle 7 in Article 2 says this principle "shall not prejudice the application of enforcement measures under Chapter VII"—a chapter that calls for the use of force by the UN when and if peaceful measures to settle a dispute are exhausted. No wonder then that the UN has been able to send only unarmed observation soldiers who stand helpless when disputes transform into armed conflicts. What's more, the UN has no Army that is geared for these purposes. Consequently, there are certain regional wars that have erupted where the UN finds itself helpless. Although the international community announced in the original charter that it was "determined" to end wars, and although it has succeeded to some measure in achieving this goal, many regional wars, disputes, and conflicts that the world has witnessed after those two major wars, and is still witnessing, are no less devastating, especially as they endure. Such developments put the Purposes and Principles found in Chapter One into question. Some of these wars, disputes, and conflicts are fought by proxy and sometimes by the participation of some regional and international powers.

What is stipulated in Article 47(2) aggravates the situation as "The Military Staff Committee shall consist of the Chief of Staff of the permanent members of the Security Council or their representatives" because the decision-making process in relation to international peacekeeping will risk reflecting national hegemonic connotations of the big influential powers in the world. Furthermore, the obligation of all members of the United Nations to provide armed forces, assistance, and facilities that is called for by Article 45 does not make things easier, as the state from which the UN asks assistance will weigh that request against its national interests and that of its allies and friends, which in turn might not tally with that of other states. The world peacekeeping operations at present are far from being satisfactory, and that leaves a lot to be desired regarding the application of Articles 25, 48, and 49, which outline the mandatory nature of UN Security Council decisions.

One has only to review the present trouble spots around the world to note that although many relevant resolutions have been taken by the UN Security Council in its peacekeeping mandate, the parties concerned have treated them with neglect, which explains why regional wars, conflicts, and disputes endure with no end in sight. Examples are found in the Western Sahara conflict, the Palestinian Question, the DRC dispute, the Cyprus question, and the enclave of Nagorno-Karabakh, to name only a few.

If member states do not adhere to and apply the council's decisions, the UN may resort to civil sanctions, and if that proves insufficient, it might use military force as called for by Articles 41 and 42. The former article gives the parties concerned and the UN a chance of not using force immediately, so civil sanctions are attempted at first, like economic, communication, and diplomatic severance. If these non-violent measures prove to be unfruitful, the use of military means mentioned in Article 42 becomes the last resort to try to solve the problem. However, sanctions have negative effects if they are applied indiscriminately to a country. There should be a distinction in that application so that sanctions should only hurt the regime of that country and should not in any way cause harm to innocent civilians. It was only recently that the UN practice of applying sanctions to all for so many years went under review by the organization. The UN Security Council arranged several working luncheons at which its members discussed this problem. The result of those meetings, which stressed the necessity of sparing innocent civilians from the fallout of sanctions, was on the table of the council's president for the month of November 1998. Finally, the council merely "took note of it." That means that the council did not adopt any resolution regarding a mandatory distinction between the guilty and the innocent when imposing sanctions. However, following that date, the UN has always had that distinction in mind, and that was the main idea and purpose.

When the charter deals with amendments to it, one cannot help but feel confused when the text in Article 108 says amendments will apply to all members of the United Nations, but also says the amendments need to be ratified according to the constitutional processes of those same members. It makes more sense to make the whole exercise within and under the auspices of the UN as an international organization and a true representative of multinationalism. National constitutions and procedures vary from one country to another and are thus limited in representation to the country's borders.

Article 23 spells out the names of the permanent member countries of the Security Council. However, two of those members have changed in form and essence: the Union of Soviet Socialist Republics was dissolved and became the present Russian Federation, with the allied countries of the former USSR becoming independent members of the UN. The second member, the Republic of China (ROC), is still there in the text, but in reality the People's Republic of China (PRC) replaced the ROC as a member state of the UN in 1971. Neither of these name changes is reflected in the article, and neither of these states has a vested interest in pursuing an amendment in the article, since both the USSR and the ROC are permanent members and have a veto, whereas the new countries might not have that veto power. Amending the article to reflect a current reality has serious historical connotations.

Articles 97 to 101 talk about the UN Secretariat, with Article 97 stipulating that the secretary-general "shall be the chief administrative officer of the Organization." In fact, the secretary-general is more than an administrative officer. It is true that the person in this role heads the UN Secretariat, but he is not dealing only with employees, their recruitment, payroll, and retirement like the average administrator does. He is asked by all major organs of the UN, including and above all, the Security Council and the General Assembly, to report on all important matters that are international in nature, including politics. His reports are important because they set the required depth and pace for solutions and resolutions to be taken by the General Assembly, Security Council, and ECOSOC. These reports are of special importance to UN member states that are limited in geography and influence on the international stage because those states do not have sufficient means and personnel to deal with and analyze the intricate issues that the UN is mandated to handle.

The adjective "administrative" is hardly indicative of the wide and varied functions that the secretary-general undertakes in the name of the organization. Finally, Article 31 of the charter permits any UN member who is not a member of the Security Council to participate in the discussion of the council when that member's interests are affected. The problem is that the council's discussions take place in a stuffy, small room which does not admit non-members. The permission given to the latter is restricted to public meetings of the council in the Chamber. At these public meetings, there is no proper discussion. Statements are read publicly, but the decisions reflected in those statements are in fact taken by council members in the small discussion room. This procedure means that the interests of non-council members are often not taken as seriously as the Member representatives, or even the UN itself, wish them to be. This is why the recommendations for the council to open its work to all UN members become quite pertinent and more democratic. After all, the Security Council is responsible for keeping peace around the world through the mechanisms of the whole UN System.

Three Eras in World Affairs

After the Allied forces defeated the Axis in the Second World War, the world saw a split in the victorious side into two distinct camps: the West, led by the United States of America, and the Communist Bloc, under the leadership of the then Soviet Union. This produced a situation commonly called the Cold War, which really amounted to fighting without weapons. Instead of weapons, the two sides used misinformation, espionage, and dirty tricks emanating from the respective ideologies of the two camps.

Oddly enough, this situation of having competing and contradictory ideologies pitted against each other benefited the United Nations System and allowed it to solve some of the world's problems that had been entrusted to the United Nations. At the height of the Cold War, this led to a situation where one side would say "yes" while the other said "no" to almost anything the other suggested. This meant that the UN found itself playing a conciliatory role, which boosted its importance and position in solving some, but not all, of the compelling international problems. A case in point is the important and decisive role played by the United Nations through the untiring efforts of its second secretary-general, Dag Hammarskjöld, which resulted in preventing the secession of two important regions in the DRC, namely Katanga and South Kasai. This marked success did not come without a heavy price—Hammarskjöld lost his life when his small aircraft crashed near Ndola, Zambia, in the middle of the negotiations. However, his efforts ultimately kept the boundaries of the DRC intact. Secretary-General Hammarskjöld is also credited for establishing for the first time what was termed the United Nations' Emergency Force (UNEF), sending its components of observer soldiers to keep the peace in various trouble spots in the world, thus confirming the United Nations' presence in the field. The observer soldiers were provided by member states that are usually neutral in their foreign policies. In the Secretariat, he established, also for the first time, some codes of conduct and regulations that guaranteed the neutrality of the international civil servant, away from influences that emanated from the capital of his or her country. In the atmosphere of the existence of two distinct competing camps during the Cold War, his attempts at the neutrality of his staff had a chance of application in the United Nations Tower and the field much more during the Cold War than after it.

The aftermath of the Cold War saw the complete disintegration of the Soviet Union and resulted in nearly all its satellite countries in Eastern Europe becoming independent countries and joining, one by one, the European Union. The result is the dissolution of the Eastern Camp and the emergence of the Western Camp and a new world order with a single, monopolar camp dominating international politics. Consequently, the balance of power has tilted toward the West, reflecting on the work of the Security Council to a certain extent a new era. The resulting imbalance has diminished the power of the secretary-general to play the role of a mediator and to advocate peaceful solutions to world problems.

The aftermath of the Cold War has even produced confrontations between the secretary-general and the influential powers, especially the veto holders whose powers are sustained by permanent membership in the council. The sixth secretary-general of the UN, Boutros Boutros-Ghali, an Egyptian veteran and experienced diplomat, became a victim of this post-Cold War transformation of the secretary-general's ability to handle world affairs. Boutros-Ghali was elected for his first term in a normal way, even getting an absolute majority in the vote. During his first term as secretary-general, the trouble spots in the world were the ones he inherited from his predecessors—internal wars in Rwanda, Angola, Yugoslavia, and Zambia, among others. His management of UN affairs was satisfactory, and he even introduced a project called "An Agenda for Peace" that suggested ways and means to solve world problems in a peaceful manner. When the time came for him to be elected to a second term as secretary-general, he again obtained the required majority of votes in the General Assembly—except this time the United States of America, a veto holder, objected to the renewal of his mandate. What happened was that in early April 1996, the 1993 ceasefire agreement between Hezbollah and Israel broke down. As a result of the renewed fighting, on April 14 of that year, 745 Lebanese civilians took refuge at the United Nations compound in Qana that housed observer soldiers affiliated with the United Nations Interim Force in Lebanon (UNIFIL). On April 18, the Israeli artillery bombarded the compound, killing 106 civilians and injuring a further 116. Secretary-General Boutros-Ghali appointed Franklin Van Kappen, the Dutch major-general, to investigate the attack. He concluded in his report that "it is unlikely that the shelling of the United Nations compound was the result of gross technical and/or procedural errors."[5] In other words, the attack was planned.

The secretary-general sided with his appointed general and refused to withdraw the latter's report despite pressure on him to do so and the consequent US opposition to his candidacy for a second term unless he withdrew the report. This confrontation between the secretary-general and one influential member of the Security Council not only weakened the necessary cooperation that should exist between the two sides, but it also undermined the independence and freedom of the secretary-general to do his job in a productive atmosphere. Boutros-Ghali's refusal to withdraw the report ultimately led the United States to veto his appointment to a second term. If there is any lesson to be drawn from that confrontation, it is that it signaled the beginning of a post-Cold War era in which a monopolar power exercised its determination to shape its influence in the way things are done in the council and the United Nations in general. This has been evident in the way subsequent secretary-generals have managed UN affairs in that they have made sure that their management did not contradict the policies and tendencies of the influential members of the council, especially the veto holders. This phenomenon has resulted in the dwindling influence and power of the subsequent secretaries-general, who could no longer use the rivalry of the two Cold War camps to their advantage. This of course means subduing the international interest represented by multinationalism in favor of the nationalism of the emerging powers. Naturally, there are exceptions to the rule—for instance, what the Russian Federation is doing in Syria, but this activity takes place under the watchful eyes of the United States and its allies.

The Present Situation

Since 1945, there have been no major world wars, and the world has seen major economic and social development, beginning with the reconstruction efforts to erase the damage caused by the two world wars. The veto power of the Allied victors is a remnant from the League of Nations and even though there was a lull in using it, no one should overlook the fact that there are two sides to this coin: while it has helped prevent a major war, using the veto and the threat to veto both have had a negative effect on the work of the Security Council. Britain, France, and China rarely use their veto; however, the United States routinely vetoes when it sees that council decisions will have negative repercussions for its close ally, Israel.

The Russian Federation rarely casts vetoes, but we have seen lately that it will not hesitate to do so when its interests are threatened, or those of its allies. Take for instance its acquired position in Syria, which realized the Federation's longtime dream of reaching the "warm waters." A draft resolution for a peaceful solution to the conflict in Syria was presented to the council. That draft was not to the liking of Russia nor its allied regime, so the Russian delegate in the council used the veto seven times to prevent the passing of the draft with its amendments, and he succeeded in annulling it. The main mandate of the United Nations System is to maintain international peace and security, essential for economic and social development, and when peace is shattered, development stagnates.

It is true that there are no major wars at present in the world, but a quick look at the atlas shows that local and regional disputes are causing enduring instability in the world. Some of these wars have been going on for a good while, like those in DRC, Rwanda, the Sahara, FARC in Colombia, Palestine, the Koreas, and Nagorno-Karabakh. Moreover, the situation in the Middle East and North Africa is especially volatile owing to the richness of oil reserves and the strategic location of these regions; fighting has been going on in Syria, Iraq, and Yemen, not to mention the volatile situation in Libya. These disputes, conflicts, and local wars are a costly affair since the resources, both natural and financial, are spent to acquire the necessary armament to feed the fighting at the expense of economic and social development.

For example, one could ask what the financial cost of the war in Syria is to the Russian government, as it maintains a sizable military presence in the country; or of the cost to government of the coalition headed by the United States; or to the Turks that are present in and around the borders of the country, busy fighting other Kurds; or to the Iranians who are also helping the regime. The same thing could be said about instability in Iraq after allowing for the difference in details. Where does this put the United Nations mandate to ensure international peace and security that is a prerequisite for development? A neutral observer will see that the United Nations' attitude toward these local and regional wars is at best timid and unsatisfactory, and through no fault of its own.

The Security Council tried hard to bring stability to Syria, but the Russian veto meant that their attempts failed despite amending the comprehensive peace resolution seven times in an effort to placate that permanent member. The people of Syria and its surrounding region have suffered the consequences. The same thing could be said about other conflicts and wars and the expected similar attitudes of other influential powers in the council. What is the catch? Is it that the armament trade cannot be justified without the existence of trouble spots? Or is it the acquisition of natural resources or the strategic location of the areas in question? Or is it all of the above? At this point in time neither the United Nations nor its secretary-general has either the willingness or the stamina to exert the required influence to change the course of events in a positive way.

Considering what is happening, one cannot avoid arriving at the conclusion that United Nations multilateralism fell victim to state nationalism.

In the General Assembly session held in New York in September 2021, the secretary-general of the United Nations delivered a comprehensive speech in which he warned of indications of a new Cold War. Maybe he was trying to refer to the present rivalry, military and economic, that is being noticed between the United States and China. The two powers have faced off militarily in the South China Sea and constantly compete over the ability to do business in the rest of the world. On the other hand, the rivalry between the United States and Russia continues. These indications are increasingly noticeable, but only time will tell if they take the shape of the Cold War that succeeded the end of the Second World War.

On a more positive note, the influential countries in the world seem to agree on a positive approach on the subject of global warming prior to the environmental summit to be held in Scotland (UK) in Fall 2021. If we can say that summit produced positive results, it would be the first time in the history of the United Nations whereby its multilateralism will be served and realized by an international mechanism instead of a nationalism methodology based on national interests, as has been the case until now, even if perspectives have shifted at subsequent summits.

Notes

1 At the time of independence in 1960, the country was called the Republic of Congo—Leopoldville to distinguish it from its neighbor, another recently independent country called the Republic of Congo—Brazzaville. The name was changed in 1971 to Zaïre, and in 1997, the name of the country changed again to the Democratic Republic of Congo, the name by which it is formally known today. It is commonly referred to as the DR Congo or simply DRC to distinguish it from its neighbor, the Republic of Congo.

2 Anthony Banbury, "I Love the U.N., but It Is Failing," *New York Times* (March 18, 2016).

3 Charlene Mires, *Capital of the World: The Race to Host the United Nations*. 5th ed. New York: NYU Press, 2019, 3.

4 "UNhappy Birthday on the UN 75th Anniversary," *The Economist Special Report* (June 20–6, 2020).

5 Franklin van Kappen, "Report Dated May 1, 1996 of the Secretary-General's Military Adviser Concerning the Shelling of the United Nations Compound at Qana on April 18, 1996."

2

The Main Organs and Specialized Agencies of the United Nations

Like any charter in any organization, Chapter Three, Article 7 of the UN Charter mentions the six main organs that constitute the core body of the organization. It is not clear why the charter equates the sixth organ, the Secretariat, with the other five, since it is the executing arm of the latter. Paragraph 2 of the same article opens the door for forming subsidiaries that should be in the service of the main organs. There is nothing that limits these organs and subsidiaries from maintaining peace and promoting development in the world. On the contrary, the wording of paragraph 2 is quite vague, thus paving the way for the emergence of scores of funds, commissions, committees, and programs. Considering the size of the organization, overlapping was to be expected. However, whenever power politics comes into play, and the veto power comes up, the claim is made that the UN would be breaching its mandate. It is therefore useful to understand what exactly the UN mandate encompasses by looking at what the main organs and the specialized agencies do.

The Main Organs

The General Assembly

The General Assembly is the largest organ in the System and includes representatives from every one of the 193 member states. The Assembly is a comprehensive arena in which members have the chance to air their opinions on every matter and item that the United Nations deals with, including racism, intolerance, inequality, climate change, poverty, hunger, and conflict.

The Assembly opens its annual meeting on the third Tuesday of September each year at the United Nations headquarters in New York City. Sessions run intensely until December and then start up again in January and continue until all business on the agenda has been dealt with. The agenda generally has more than 100 items that take up a variety of subjects referred to above. The meeting is presided over by a president, who is elected for one year. Often, a session runs through until right before the opening of the next session the following September. The president oversees the application of the resolutions taken by the Assembly, among other things, in a special bureau at the United Nations headquarters, where he meets delegates all year round before he hands over the presidency to the new president at the next session.

The president of the General Assembly, through efforts of his country, tries as much as possible to introduce a new subject, procedure, or meeting related to the mandate of the United Nations in order to leave a distinctive mark of achievement. For example, a president might try to arrange international conferences on relevant subjects like climate change, disarmament, and drugs.

The period from September to December is the most intense working period, and delegations travel from various capitals around the world to attend. The first and second weeks are topped by the presence of heads of state, prime ministers, and foreign ministers from the member states, who deliver speeches that reflect their countries' opinions and stances on various agenda items before the Assembly.

Meticulous preparation goes into the respective speeches. The longest speech to date was delivered in the 1957 session by India's V.K. Menon: it lasted for eight hours and covered the dispute with Pakistan on the region of Kashmir; the shortest usually comes in the form of a single-page delivery by the foreign minister of the United Kingdom. After the first two weeks, the hall of the Assembly empties as delegates disperse to participate in the Assembly's six main committees, which deal successively with disarmament and international security (First Committee); economy and financial affairs (Second Committee); social, humanitarian, and cultural affairs (Third Committee); special political issues and decolonization (Fourth Committee); organization, administrative, and budget affairs (Fifth Committee); and legal issues (Sixth Committee). The committees' meetings run parallel to the Assembly's general debate, while the recommendations of the six main committees are brought to the Assembly so that members can vote on them.

It should be noted that the General Assembly resolutions are not binding on member states. Even though the permanent delegations of member states in New York City are numerically enriched by delegates from their respective capitals, some of the smaller delegations cannot afford to be present at all concurrent meetings, so they are forced to rely on documents prepared by the Secretariat, which makes it more than simply an administrative outfit. In the end, the General Assembly is a forum with nonbinding resolutions, where delegations can speak their mind on various issues dealt with in the United Nations that are of interest, and at times need, to its member states. It is especially relevant to needy, helpless, and uninfluential members who find in the multilateralism of the United Nations a refuge from opportunist states and institutions that might hook them with debts and unfair utilization of their resources. However, this talk about the General Assembly and the United Nations is idealistic because things on the ground are different and not as rosy as this picture might suggest. Even the bilateral meetings held between delegates on the side do not escape national interests, though they sometimes touch on the General Assembly's agenda items.

Debates in the General Assembly can drag well into the night owing to the rule of procedure known as "The Right of Reply," whereby any member of the Assembly is allowed to voice their objection to the opinion of the representative of another state. This cycle can continue almost indefinitely. Examples are found in the exchanges between the delegates of the two Koreas, the Israeli delegate and the Palestinian Observer, Moroccan and Algerian delegates and Polisario Representative, or Cypriot and Turkish delegates—the delegates of the two Koreas are particularly noted for exchanging replies for a long time. It is tiring listening to these exchanges after a long working day filled with speeches and participation in debates. Not only are delegates' concentrations flagging, but they are also aware that they must prepare detailed reports about their participation in the General Assembly session.

The COVID-19 pandemic coincided with the seventy-fifth anniversary of the founding of the UN. It was a perfect opportunity for delegates from around the world to debate this calamity at the United Nations General

Assembly and to find a unified international approach and solution. Instead, we encountered reports of scattered, unproductive accounts of how different nations dealt with the pandemic that resulted in enormous fatalities across waves of the virus.

The Security Council

The Security Council is the most powerful of the main organs in the United Nations System, outstripping the importance even of the International Court of Justice housed in The Hague in the Netherlands. Since there are many security councils in many member states, this particular council should properly be called the International Security Council, but people have grown used to referring to it without the "international" part, especially when they talk about the United Nations. Apart from the permanent five members who are part of the Security Council for life or until genuine reform of the United Nations System is introduced, being a non-permanent member in the council is one of the most important aspirations of all United Nations member states. The competition for membership is fierce, active, and alive because the number of non-permanent members in the council is a meager 10 compared to the total United Nations membership of 193. It is not only prestigious to be in the council, but it is also important for members to be able to participate in the discussions of the most powerful body of the System where decisions are taken that will shape the course of actions that the United Nations will take on an international level. The resolutions passed by the Security Council affect many countries since the council's resolutions are binding for the whole membership. That's why the elections to the Security Council have been regulated and organized by the General Assembly in which they take place.

Nominations for membership of the Security Council come from five geographical groups that were set up by the Assembly. Each group has an allocated number of seats in the council: three for Africa, two for Asia and the Pacific, two for Latin America and the Caribbean, one for Eastern Europe, and two for Western Europe and Other States. Ideally, each regional group endorses the required number of candidates to fill the number of seats allocated to them when the voting takes place in the Assembly, but this is not always how it plays out. Since voting takes place at the Assembly, where votes are assigned to the countries and not to these geographic groups, individual countries can present nominations to the council from the floor. As a result, there have been instances where a country that was not part of the nominating groups put forward their own candidate in addition to those endorsed by the group representatives, which leads to an election rather than a ratification. Neither the phenomenon of having five permanent members of the council nor the highly disproportional number of the non-permanent members compared to the total membership of the United Nations reflects positively on the efficiency of the council in fulfilling its mandate. Both the procedure for establishing membership of the council and the composition of the council are flawed, and this has a direct impact on the ability of the council to respond to crises.

The original composition of the Security Council was wrong from the start. A setup that discriminates between members both in the duration of membership and in the weight of their vote has complicated the council's functioning. The makeup of the Security Council has invited members, especially the Permanent Five, to prioritize their national interests over international interests. The Permanent Five do not hesitate to interfere in the mandate of the UN. This interference and the flawed design of the council have led to an inability to respond to crises in effective ways, although there have been notable successes. The 1991 liberation of Kuwait from Iraqi occupation is a bright positive example. On the other hand, the US invasion of Iraq in 2003, which was not sanctioned by the council, was a disaster that left the Middle East in enduring turmoil.

The Economic and Social Council (ECOSOC)

This is the organ that was mandated with seeing that reconstruction happened in devastated Europe after the Second World War; later it became responsible for development, economic and social, in all member states all over the world. The ECOSOC is mandated by Article 55 of the charter to ensure the coordination of economic and social fields of the United Nations by promoting a higher standard of living in the member states, by realizing full employment, and finding solutions to the problems of health, education, culture, and communication, as well as by encouraging respect for human rights. ECOSOC has fifty-four members who are at the same time members of the United Nations and who are elected in and by the General Assembly for a period of three years. Like the setup in the Security Council, elections to the ECOSOC are based on the number of seats allocated to each of the five United Nations geographical groups: fourteen seats are allocated to Africa, eleven to Asia, six to Eastern Europe, ten to Latin America and the Caribbean, and thirteen to Western Europe and Other States. It is worth noting that all five permanent members of the Security Council are presently elected to the ECOSOC and provide much of its budget.

The ECOSOC is the largest and most complex organ of the United Nations System. It carries out a range of activities that span a wide spectrum and diversified fields relating to economic and social development. For this far-reaching purpose, it has established fourteen major specialized agencies to ensure the well-being of almost all facets of human life among citizens in member states. In addition, it has scores of commissions, committees, and bodies under its supervision to carry out and report on their work.

The specialized agencies are: International Labour Organization (ILO), Food and Agriculture Organization of the United Nations (FAO), United Nations Educational, Scientific and Cultural Organization (UNESCO), World Health Organization (WHO), World Bank Group, International Monetary Fund (IMF), International Civil Aviation Organization (ICAO), World Meteorological Organization (WMO), International Maritime Organization (IMO), International Telecommunication Union (ITU), Universal Postal Union (UPU), World Intellectual Property Organization (WIPO), International Fund for Agricultural Development (IFAD), United Nations Industrial Development Organization (UNIDO), and the World Tourism Organization (WTO).

Among the other bodies and organs that report to the ECOSOC other than the specialized agencies, there are certain funds and programs that are worth mentioning owing to their size and importance, and thus their contributions to the mandate of the United Nations. These are: United Nations Children's Fund (UNICEF), United Nations Conference on Trade and Development (UNCTAD), United Nations Fund for Women, United Nations Development Programme (UNDP), United Nations Environment Programme (UNEP), the Office of the United Nations Commissioner for Refugees

(UNHCR), United Nations Population Fund (UNFPA), United Nations Relief and Works Agency for Palestinian Refugees in Near East (UNRWA), Office for Drug Control and Crime Prevention (ODCCP), World Food Programme (WFP), and UN-HABITAT.

The International Court of Justice (ICJ)

The ICJ (sometimes referred to as the "World Court") is the legal arm of the United Nations System. Housed in The Hague, the World Court is the only one of the six main organs of the United Nations that is found outside New York City. Its mandate is to settle disputes among United Nations member states, which may cover matters relating to borders and territorial waters by applying principles of international law. The World Court's second mandate is to investigate legal matters referred to it by the United Nations' main organs as well as the specialized agencies, and that includes resolutions taken. Furthermore, in recent years, the World Court has made it its job to try world leaders who have been accused of committing crimes against humanity—from the Balkan wars to the Sudan conflicts. The World Court is run by fifteen judges elected by the General Assembly and the Security Council.

In the election of judges for the ICJ at the Security Council, no distinction is made between permanent and non-permanent members of the council, according to Paragraph 2 of Article 10 of the charter. However, one should not rule out the political influence of big powers on the judicial decisions of the court. Take the example of cases against leaders who committed crimes against humanity. We enter here into the realm of state sovereignty. Article 10 cannot force the state of which the accused is a national to hand over the incumbent. Many persons who took part in the Bosnian massacres are free, away from the judgment of the court. However, Article 10 has marked some successful resolutions of conflicts when it comes to border disputes among member states.

The Trusteeship Council

The council was established in 1945 according to Article 75 of the United Nations Charter for the purpose of supervising eleven colonies as they passed from the stage of being colonized to gradual independence. In 1994, the United Nations mandate represented by this council was accomplished, and the council indefinitely suspended its activities. The territories in question were: Western Samoa, Tanganyika, Rwanda-Urundi (later Rwanda-Burundi), Cameroon (British), Cameroon (French), Togoland (British), Togoland (French), New Guinea, Nauru, Strategic Trust Territory/Trust Territory of the Pacific Islands, and Italian Somaliland.

Article 77 states that the council's trusteeship would extend to "territories now held under mandate," which covered those territories under League of Nations mandates.[1] Of these, several territories were included in the scope of the Trusteeship Council. The Strategic Trust Territory/Trust Territory of the Pacific Islands included the territories that had been assigned to Japan under the League of Nations' South Seas Mandate. The mandate for Palestine was considered complete in May 1948, even though only half that mandate was fulfilled, and it was therefore not included among the Trusteeship Council mandates. The one territory that was not included in this list of Trusteeship Council mandates was Southwest Africa (now Namibia)—South Africa had proposed that rather than continue to administer the territory as a mandate, it should be allowed to annex it. The international community opposed this move, and in 1950, the ICJ ruled that South Africa continued to have mandatory obligations regarding the territory. Namibia eventually gained independence in 1990.

It is not normal to establish a major organ in an important organization to help occupied territories gain independence and later say that the organ's mandate has ceased to be necessary. Also, nothing in Chapter Twelve establishes that the Trusteeship Council relates to the abrupt stoppage. There remain a fair number of territories in the world that were occupied because of major or local wars. Referenda are sometimes organized in those territories that aspire to statehood. The Falkland Islands, Puerto Rico, and Nouméa and New Caledonia are a few examples of places that still aspire for statehood. The UN has a positive record in keeping Kosovo away from and in the middle of massacres. I would argue that the UN Trusteeship Council is needed now more than ever before. It is just that the states that have direct or indirect influence on those territories resist their handling by the UN, notwithstanding the cost incurred by those states. It is a forlorn conclusion that the Trusteeship Council still has a lot of potential work that is barred by dysfunction.

The Secretariat

The sixth and last organ of the United Nations, the Secretariat, is the executive branch where all resolutions of the General Assembly, the Security Council, and the ECOSOC are transformed into actions by member states. Considering that there are 193 member states, one can only imagine the colossal amount of work that this executive branch undertakes and the necessary number of personnel and expense that this entails, not to mention the office space required. What's more, this executive branch has the important task of preparing for the various meetings, conferences, and seminars held by the United Nations, including producing all the documentation that accompanies these events. It is estimated that the Secretariat alone employs more than 40,000 staff members in its offices around the world, including its headquarters.

The Secretariat is dealt with in Chapter Fifteen of the charter. Article 97 implies that the Secretariat will be headed by a secretary-general and that "He shall be the chief administrative officer of the Organization." This is an understatement because Article 98 notes that he performs other functions entrusted to him by the General Assembly, the Security Council, and the ECOSOC. Much of the work under Article 98 is political rather than administrative. If it is not clear enough yet that the secretary-general is more than an administrative officer, Article 99 spells out that he may bring to the attention of the Security Council any matter that may be a threat to international peace and security. If that is not political, what is? The secretary-general is in fact more of a political agent than an administrative one. He, together with his staff, not only convenes meetings of the principal organs of the United Nations but also produces the material for discussion; he participates in discussions when asked to and certainly follows up on the outcomes of these debates and incorporates this information in subsequent meetings. In between all this, the secretary-general initiates contact with and mediates between the concerned parties to facilitate arriving at a solution that is acceptable to all. This comprehensive and far-reaching work surpasses administration to include politics, be it developmental or peacekeeping. The work of the secretary-general and his personnel is sensitive and indispensable to the operation of the UN.

Article 100 of the charter refers to the integrity and neutrality of the secretary-general and his staff, stressing loyalty only to the organization, away from any interference by member states that might tarnish that neutrality. In the history of the United Nations, there have been instances where that neutrality was put to critical test. U Thant was the secretary-general in 1967 when Egypt's Gamal Abdel Nasser asked him to withdraw the United Nations Observatory Troops stationed between the Israelis and the Egyptians in Sinai. Immense pressure was put on him not to adhere to the requests by several member states, headed by the United States of America. A few of his senior officers also followed the suggestion of non-withdrawal, surely influenced by their governments and forgetting Article 100 of the charter regarding the neutrality of international civil servants. Finally, U Thant acknowledged Egypt's demand as a host country of the United Nations troops and approved their withdrawal. It is an example of the utmost importance and independence of the post that the secretary-general has acquired over the years, both in theory and in practice, highlighting the political rather than the administrative nature of his responsibilities.

The Specialized Agencies

The specialized agencies are part of the executive arm of the ECOSOC, which plans action for development in various fields and according to the needs of member states. The agencies implement these plans. The agencies' activities are supported by several functional standing and regional commissions, standing committees, ad hoc and expert bodies, and funds and programs. One can imagine by the sheer number of these organizations the size, importance, and financial burden of the ECOSOC and its affiliates.

The "Big Five" specialized agencies were formed right after the Second World War on, or immediately after the establishment of the United Nations in 1945. These original agencies were the Bretton Woods Institutions (World Bank and the IMF), the United Nations Educational, Scientific, and Cultural Organization

(UNESCO); the World Health Organization (WHO); the International Labour Organization (ILO); and the Food and Agricultural Organization (FAO). Their respective headquarters are in Washington, Paris, Geneva (for WHO and ILO), and Rome. The urgency of their establishment reflects the need to cover the basic needs of human beings in the aftermath of a devastating war, i.e., money, food, lodging, and health. All the Big Five are essential agencies, but perhaps the one that has a direct impact on a human being is his housing and education. Housing and education are the responsibility of UNESCO, while birth and health fall under the auspices of the United Nations Children's Fund (UNICEF), a fund that reports to the ECOSOC.

UNICEF is probably the most popular of all the United Nations Organizations, largely because of the work done by its goodwill ambassadors, who are chosen from the art celebrities like singers and movie stars. It is true that the United Nations and its other organizations have envoys here and there, but information about them does not go beyond the circles of their specializations while the celebrities of UNICEF are known all over the world. Their fame brings moral and material support to the Fund.

The Significance of the Location of the Agencies

It sounds totally logical for the United Nations proper and its financial institutions to be housed in the United States of America because the United States took on the burden of supporting expenses necessary to repair the damage in Europe caused by the devastating Second World War under the Marshall Plan (European Economic Recovery Plan). It also seems appropriate that nearly all the specialized agencies should be headquartered in Europe because that is where the reconstruction took place. It makes sense, too, that the agencies became established in Europe given the European know-how in development; however, that is the historical reality. Since the 1940s and 1950s, the world, including the developing countries, has acquired experience with development and the focal points for development have shifted away from Europe and the solution that worked after the Second World War—to have the agencies located on the ground where development is needed—no longer applies. A problem in Mozambique cannot be dealt with from the comfort of

Geneva, just as post-war Europe's problems could not be dealt with effectively from America.

The headquarters of nearly all the agencies are in the West. Some might argue that these Western-based international headquarters have field offices in the developing countries where the problems are dealt with, but what is the use of that when all major decisions are taken in American, Canadian, and European countries? It is high time and for the benefit of the developing countries they are serving, that an effective decentralization of these agencies occurs, especially when it comes to the decision-making process so that with time power of action will be gradually transferred to the field offices. It is an economical and efficient way to solve the problems in the developing countries in Asia, Africa, and Latin America. It also constitutes less of a burden on those countries when it comes to paying their annual or biannual dues to the United Nations and its affiliated organizations, institutions, and funds.

Bretton Woods Institutions

There are two distinct financial institutions in the United Nations System: the World Bank Group and the IMF. The former deals with loans for development, while the latter undertakes the task of regulating and stabilizing member states' currencies. The World Bank, as the name indicates, is a bank in the strict sense of the word. Certain countries that can afford it have shares in that bank and hence their votes in the bank's Board of Directors determine the availability of the loans other member states seek for their economic and social development.

Strictly speaking, the Bretton Woods Institutions do not operate on a for-profit basis, as any other bank would, and the World Bank is lenient in imposing interest rates on needy recipients. This all sounds good in theory; however, in practice the large amount of funds at its disposal makes it a kind of "club riche." Recipients of World Bank funds are mostly governments and their leaders. The drawback of this tendency might be that some of them use part of the loan in building white elephants in or around their birthplace. On the other hand, one cannot rule out the possibility of political maneuvers in favor of members who have many shares in the bank. If this happens, it will have an adverse effect on the process of lending. As to the IMF, it comes to the rescue of recipients whose economies are passing through turbulence by regulating their currencies. However, there may be some strings attached to this practice: The currencies are eventually devaluated and goods subsidies are lifted, among other things. This causes hardship to the people of those countries whose governments are dealing with the IMF. One could conclude that these ultra-rich institutions are dealing with desperate governments and people and consequently relations between the two sides ultimately become less normal and humane.

If one country asks another to provide experts in certain fields of development, there is a possibility that strings might be attached. The country providing support might, through the advice of an expert, try to influence the way things are done in the receiving country. Further, that expert might bring in other experts from his country. Also, the providing country may steer the assistance to serve its own needs. Lastly, the cost of the expert is often higher than that provided by the specialized agencies of the UN. With the UN, you are sure to get its assistance free of charge and you do not have to fear any interference in your own affairs, political or otherwise.

In other words, in their own way, the Bretton Woods Institutions are no less powerful than the Permanent Five. The problem is that they cannot strike up direct dialogue with people at the grass roots, the ones who are intended to be the ultimate beneficiaries of their economic development projects. These institutions deal with governments, and the projects they fund have to be officially sanctioned, which opens the structures and mechanisms of the projects to many influences that put the desired outcome at risk of corruption, delays, and overlap.

Many oversized, unnecessary projects have been built that are similar to existing ones. The idea should be to build developmental projects that are complementary to each other and not rival each other. Sovereignty is no excuse. Projects should fall under the auspices of the UN, not left to the mercy of the World Bank, and be directed to the benefit of homogeneous regions rather than individual countries. For example, regions should build universities in such a way that one will specialize in Medicine for the whole region, while another university does the same for Engineering.

Conclusion

These institutions working independently, as they do, pose a challenge to the effectiveness of the UN System in its entirety. They are part of the system, and are formal parts of the structure, but they operate separately with their own purposes and priorities. This contradictory situation poses a serious problem, with a group of financial institutions working on their own, geared toward generating profits for their shareholders, while freely ignoring the humanitarian objectives of the broader UN System. Bringing the Bretton Woods Institutions directly under the administration of the UN is not, of course, a panacea. One obvious challenge is that donor states might be less generous when they have less control over how donated funds are used and if they have less control over the financial and monetary policies of the states who are receiving funds. At the same time, the donor states also tend to have the upper hand in shaping the decisions made by other parts of the United Nations, as we will see in Chapter 3.

Note

1 "UN Trusteeship Council Documentation," Dag Hammarskjöld Library, https://research.un.org/en/docs/tc/territories.

3

Performance of the United Nations Economic and Social Response

The United Nations' assistance for development in its member states is a shy, timid exercise because the program is not known except to those countries that benefit from it. This situation bars other member states from benefiting from the experience of realization in the field. There are many reasons for the relative anonymity of this program, including that the operations for development do not constitute "sensational" news for the general public. However, to avoid wasting resources and time when there is an overlap or a repetition of elements among projects, it is useful to know what has worked for other similar projects, and for that reason alone, everybody should have access to the operational details. Of course, individual project details are all laid out by the United Nations in well-prepared files and documents—that is not the concern here; it is the way the projects are evaluated when they pass through the various stages of execution. An additional concern is how, once a project is complete, the visible benefits of the development program to citizens of the country can be projected to and through other developing societies. The Bretton Woods United Nations financial institutions, which respectively act as a strict bank and a currency regulator, do not do much to show the success of their development assistance. Clients who seek their financial help must adhere to strict conditions of borrowing that might have negative repercussions if things go wrong. The public, when it is aware of their activities at all, mostly hears about failures, defaults, and the misuse of funds.

From the look of it, sustained by a seventy-five-year experience, the poor are getting poorer in needy United Nations member states, while those who can help from the private sector, especially the international conglomerates, are thinking only of profits for their stakeholders. It is not known if the Bretton Woods Institutions are copying them because they are an effective source of finance, and it won't affect their fat profits. It does not make sense that international financial institutions must operate like their sisters found in national governments, as each has its own unique characteristics.

Originally, the Bretton Woods Institutions, including the International Bank for Reconstruction and Development (IBRD), were established as mechanisms for reconstructing war-damaged Europe according to the vision of the Marshall Plan. With time, after the reconstruction was largely completed, these institutions reinvented themselves as full-fledged commercial entities, covering not only Europe but also the whole world. Although they work in a similar fashion to ordinary banks and commercial moneylenders, their decisions are sometimes informed by more than strict financial objectives. Consequently, they exercise political pressure as well as financial assistance, especially when it comes to lending to states rather than private entities. This is true of the International Monetary Fund (IMF), which seeks to regulate the currencies of debtor nations, as well as the World Bank and the International Development Association (IDA). This curious situation understandably concerns UN member states, including those that have and those that have not, as the former buy shares in Bretton Woods Institutions and, thereby, are able to exert a deciding influence on who to lend to and also have a say in the financial terms of these loans.

The most sensible way to avoid such political influence would be for these institutions to cease operating independently as financial institutions or as lending banks subject exclusively to the whims of shareholders. Instead, they should be part and parcel of the UN, administered as lenders to the neediest member states as an important contribution to their sustainable economic and social development. Indeed, the development part of the United Nations System comes in the form of assisting its member states in realizing their economic and social development projects by providing financial and expertise components needed in part or in whole so that those states achieve a satisfactory degree of progress for the benefit of their citizens, as opposed to further enriching the lending states or shackling borrowing states to unreasonable austerity measures.

Considering that there are 193 UN member states, international United Nations assistance is executed at a considerable cost by a considerable number of United Nations staff and experts who in turn deal with many national officials and staff of the countries concerned. Since sizable amounts of money and documents circulate and change hands, several essential elements should be scrutinized, including vigilance, integrity, efficiency, accountability, and supervision. Despite the precautions required regarding the sheer size of that developmental assistance provided by the United Nations, the record of the quality and efficiency with which the projects are realized tends to be satisfactory and beneficial.

Coordination among departments and sections is very much called for out of necessity, as major developmental projects pass through three essential stages: planning, execution, and evaluation. Unfortunately for many major projects, attention is paid mostly to planning and execution, while evaluation is often neglected. Once a project is completed, the focus shifts to the next project, and it is hard to go back and evaluate what has been done thoroughly. In the worst scenarios, certain projects will miss the advantage of evaluation altogether. Yet evaluation of a project is not a luxury because proper evaluation can prevent repetition and save money, resources, and staff. Often, a department might realize midway through that another department had engaged in a similar project and that they were duplicating efforts. The resulting wastage is significant. In the case of the United Nations System, with budgets that run into billions, evaluation becomes a must to avoid such wastage. Unfortunately, the fact that the United Nations project initiators and directors must race against time to spend the allocated budgets before the end of the year so that they can be included in the following year's budget means that there is little opportunity to reflect and evaluate.

Department heads should realize that requests for project financing come originally from member states that in turn may have shelved their national development projects to pay their dues to the United Nations and, at the same time, seek assistance from the United Nations System. Furthermore, coordination and evaluation guard against waste and misuse of financial resources. One sometimes hears about the disappearance of a couple of million dollars here and there, with no information about tracking or tracing.

In fact, the temptation is there considering the colossal budget sums and the intricate and complicated contacts between the United Nations System and its member states necessary for project realization. This does not negate the fact that the United Nations gets a positive and satisfactory note when it comes to the thousands of developmental economic and social projects that it has successfully realized in many developing countries of its member states.

One demonstrative but tiny example of a successful UN project is one realized in Bahrain, a small member state. This project was undertaken in 1980 by one of the Programs affiliated with the ECOSOC, i.e., the United Nations Development Programme (UNDP), and continues to this day. Shrimps are raised in ponds adjacent to the seashore until they have grown big enough to be released into the sea. The project acts as a regulatory process for catching shrimps for consumption and guarantees that shrimps, when caught, are mature and are the right size. A similar success story that was undertaken in the same country involves the collection of dates.

How projects are financed makes a difference to their success. The amount of funding available to member states varies and is based on cost-sharing between the United Nations and the countries concerned, with the UN and its affiliates financing the full amount in cases of some projects pertaining to needy countries. The yardstick for eligibility for assistance is the gross domestic product (GDP) of countries seeking assistance. When that assistance takes the form of loans from the United Nations financial institutions rather than the UN's direct participation in project realization, the rules of the game change. In such cases, unfortunately, multilateralism gives way to political preferences determined by the national interests of the shareholders rather than the principles of international assistance. For example, in 1956, the World Bank denied the financing required for the construction of the Aswan Dam in Egypt after the United States withdrew its investment. One of the ambitious development goals of the 1952 revolution in Egypt was to maximize the productivity of the agricultural land irrigated from the Nile River. Constructing a dam was the obvious solution. Egyptian authorities realized that the logical course of action was to apply to the Bretton Woods Institutions for financial support, as a project of such magnitude was well beyond their means. From the perspective of the United Nations, nothing would be more reasonable than a member state calling upon the organization for assistance. However, while the Bretton Woods Institutions are formally part of the UN System, they are not subject to the same rules as the rest of the System.

Consequently, when the United States—as the leading donor to the Bretton Woods Institutions—objected to the loan for apparently political reasons, the Bretton Woods Institutions obeyed. This decision precipitated the Suez Crisis when, a week later, Egypt nationalized the Suez Canal, seeking to finance the dam from the proceeds. This course of action in turn led to retaliatory military strikes on Egypt by France, Israel, and the United Kingdom. Ironically, these military actions occurred, apparently, without the knowledge or consent of the United States. Then, to prevent escalation and avoid the possible involvement of the Soviet Union in the conflict, the United States pressured its allies to withdraw their forces, leaving the Suez Canal under Egyptian sovereignty. Had the financing of the Aswan Dam project been approved, none of these lamentable events would have occurred.

There are also cases where the World Bank imposed harsh restrictions as a condition for providing the loans, like doing away with some of the subsidies the country concerned received on certain goods and services. The hardship this causes for the population in turn results in upheavals and disturbances in the country. Furthermore, because of these hardships, the country might devalue its currency, which causes the economy to deteriorate further and leads international financial institutions to decrease their rating. This unfavorable situation hardly reflects the noble and positive objectives that lie behind international assistance.

An idea to consider in these cases is transforming the United Nations financial institutions from institutions seeking profit or political gain into non-profit funds with moderate returns that should not surpass the cost of running them. This should be part of the reform that one is after to make the United Nations System function in a better way. However, despite the shortcomings that come from either the project realization departments and sections of the United Nations or the institutions that provide the financing, the achievements of the United Nations System in this endeavor are numerous, and their success certainly outweighs the shortcomings encountered along the way. Suffice it to say that the United Nations' expertise has no strings, political or otherwise, attached to it, is easier to come by, and is backed by many years of international experience.

If a country asks another to provide experts in certain fields of development, there is a possibility that strings might be attached, direct or indirect. The country providing support might, through the expert, try to influence the way things are done in the receiving country. That expert might bring in other experts from his country. Also, the providing country may steer the assistance according to its own needs, rather than the benefit of the receiving country. Lastly, the cost of the expert may be higher than the cost of one provided by the United Nations. With the UN, countries are sure to get assistance free of charge without fear of political or economic interference in domestic affairs.

It should be noted here that no institution, including those working for the social and economic development of poorer countries, is spared from political interference. However, if one attempts to make a comparison between development organizations belonging to the bilateral sector and those working multilaterally within the UN System, one can observe that the strings are fewer and less restrictive in multilateral collaborations. UN development assistance is almost free to recipient countries and is directed toward a single goal—the comprehensive well-being of the people of its member states. This is rarely true of bilateral assistance which is, for the most part, conditional on the priorities of the donors, for whom development assistance is a form of soft power. Hence, our emphasis throughout is that the Bretton Woods Institutions should be fully amalgamated within the UN System proper, rather than operate independently, as is the case at present.

Apart from the evaluation process that should be built into projects realized with the help of the United Nations System, there is a need for a feedback mechanism to evaluate how this realization made an impact on the population, whether directly or indirectly, and whether, coupled with other related projects, it resulted in a better life for the people. If that analysis is not undertaken, project realization might risk becoming scattered individual exercises and fall victim to personal, isolated tendencies characterized by the fact that decision-making reflects the interests of those who are entrusted with it.

Evaluating a project is not the end of the story, even if it was executed in a perfect way. The value of every project should be considered relative to oth identical projects, which in turn are part of shaping the perspectives at the base of an impact. Unless there is a felt impact on the lives of the people that the UN assistance targets, it will be a futile exercise. Unfortunately, there is currently no evaluation of the UN's assistance projects, and what little does occur does not go beyond figures. When there has been an evaluation, properly speaking, then there is no study to find out what positive change the assistance made on the people who were targeted. There are several reasons for this shortcoming. The size of the UN structure, coupled with the corresponding budget amounts and the staff required, does not make evaluation a given in the work of the UN. What's more, time constraints related to meeting deadlines do not make evaluating projects easy. Over time, these problems did not help to establish a culture of evaluating the impact of projects undertaken in the UN System.

An Insight into UNESCO and UNICEF

UNESCO and UNICEF deserve special attention in the context of the UN's social and economic development agenda. Taken together, these two organizations represent nearly all aspects of the development sector of the United Nations System, with mandates encompassing multiple dimensions of the life of a human being from birth to old age and death. From its inception, UNESCO has covered education, science, research, and culture in the broadest sense of these terms. Over time, information, media, and communication have been added to UNESCO's brief, and the letter C in the acronym now stands for both culture and communication, already two major fields besides education and science and technology. With such additions, UNESCO has expanded both the scope and importance of its portfolio of responsibilities, and this has resulted in significant growth in staff and budget. For its part, UNICEF is an organization that focuses on the needs of children, which includes but is not limited to health, nutrition, shelter, protection, and security, as well as education. Looking at UNESCO and UNICEF from a wider perspective, their scope and complexity almost form a miniature United Nations in their own right. UNICEF endeavors to provide nearly all the services required for a subset of the world population, namely children. Together with UNESCO, which has an equally broad set of priorities but that is not focused on a single age demographic, the organizations make a complementary happy couple in economic and social development. It should be noted that the success of UNICEF and UNESCO does not negate or deny the need for the programs and services provided by other UN organizations, although the mandates of most other subdivisions of the UN are more specialized than those of UNICEF and UNESCO.

UNESCO was founded on November 4, 1946, almost immediately after the establishment of the United Nations itself as an outcome of the International Committee on Intellectual Cooperation. In the aftermath of the Second World War, UNESCO's mandate was to advance peace, social and economic development, and human rights by facilitating collaboration and dialogue among nations. This peaceful mission after a war is emphasized in the preamble of its constitution, which says that "since wars begin in the minds of men, it is in the minds of men that the defenses of peace must be constructed." Translated into reality, the main functions of UNESCO are to ensure that every child has access to proper education, to promote cultural acceptance between nations while protecting cultural sites, to improve technology to aid in the distribution of resources and energy, and to secure the safety of individual expression and basic human rights. The first impression of the preamble and the mandate is that they are wide and varied in scope: education, cultural sites, technology, expression, safety, resources, and rights. That might explain the progressive expansion of the number of its buildings and staff, with all the mounting cost that goes with it.

UNESCO was originally housed in London, UK, and then moved to the Majestic Hotel on Avenue Kléber in Paris. There it functioned in an unfitting working environment during the twelve-year transitional period while permanent headquarters were being built. In 1958, the headquarters was moved to Paris, France, and located in UNESCO House in the seventh district at Place de Fontenoy (Fountain Square) in the City of Light.

UNESCO House was designed and built for the organization. The present headquarters has four buildings designed by three architects. The main building is constructed in the shape of the letter (Y) or "three-pointed stars" and stands on seventy-two columns, which is on its own unique. The second building has an "accordion" egg shape and was built especially for the use of the plenary session of the General Conference held every two years, which makes UNESCO's budget and program biennial. The third building is in the form of a cube, while the fourth is constituted of two sunken floors with six courtyard openings. The whole complex is a work of art, but it was soon crowded by an ever-increasing number of staff, both secretarial and professional, which made the organization think of adding a fifth building. As space was not available at the present headquarters, they had to look in the neighborhood. The functional design of this new building is a far cry from the artistic touch of the headquarters at Place de Fontenoy, where many famous artists have adorned it with several works of art that match the design. Today, these buildings act as the center of operations for more than 2,200 staff from 169 nationalities working in Paris and fifty-three field offices.[1] The cost of running the organization's program, a cost that is in part borne by a number of hard-pressed member states, is unimaginably high.

Has the organization overstretched itself with many mandates and crowded locations? Only time will tell. However, there are a couple of uneasy indications that matters are not satisfactory. How can one handle so many things with a large staff without losing track on the way? How can one promote or solve a problem of education in a developing country by taking decisions in easy-living in Paris? To solve a problem, you must feel it and live with it. The field officers will not do a satisfactory job when decisions are made in Paris, and sending someone to the country that needs assistance for a month or two to gain expertise is not a sustainable solution. Even that expertise has fallen victim to monotony and repetition. When experts return from the field to submit their reports in office X at headquarters, where the mission originated, they are often advised to transfer to office Y because there is another mission coming up in that country. Missions and reports risk becoming standard regardless of the efficient environment that exists in various developing countries. The repetition and standardization diminish the quality of the organization's missions and their reports. This unwanted phenomenon is in part the result of various UNESCO departments at headquarters having to spend their allocated budgets and their appropriations for executing their departments' programs before the year-end by hastily choosing the available experts who happen to be visiting the headquarters at the time. Since almost all experts that are sent to the field pass by the headquarters to submit their reports, chances are a qualified expert will be found simply by walking through one of the three wings of the "pointed stars" building.

To fulfill its far-reaching mandates, UNESCO also holds many workshops, seminars, meetings, and conferences. The cost of holding these meetings is usually borne by the organization, which the representative of the director-general of the organization sometimes takes as a way of controlling the procedures and recommendations. In one meeting, a representative went as far as telling the delegates that the director-general will not "like" the way the meeting is heading toward the kind of recommendations that the delegates want to suggest. The representatives of the Secretariat sometimes seem to forget that the financing of meetings, which comes from UNESCO's budget, originates from member states of the organization and that the director-general as well as the Secretariat are in the service of member states and not the other way round.

As for the working atmosphere at headquarters, it can be overbearing. Some directors-general become somewhat authoritarian, and political considerations often feature strongly. Relationships can often sour when a division head from a bigger, more influential country is deputized to someone who comes from a less influential nation. Furthermore, as many countries with limited resources do not have or cannot afford the required number of delegates that can go through the mass of printed material that comes out of the Secretariat, the latter finds other ways to supervise and control the work of the organization.

UNICEF is the United Nations fund that promotes the health and welfare of children around the world. It was, like UNESCO, founded on December 11, 1946, in the aftermath of the Second World War to provide relief and shelter to the children who were victims of that major war. Unlike many United Nations Organizations which have fixed budgets imposed by quotas and paid by member states, UNICEF is funded voluntarily by governments, organizations, foundations, the private sector, and individuals. In 2019, the organization collected a record 568 million US dollars. In contrast with UNESCO, UNICEF benefits much more from voluntary contributions from donor nations and individuals, and finding funding to finance its projects has never been a problem for UNICEF.

UNICEF has its headquarters in New York City and has seven regional offices around the world, including a supply division in Copenhagen that provides vaccines for children. The Fund is one of the most popular organizations in the world, and its scope of work covers 190 countries. Its operations are run and controlled by an Executive Board, and the director-general is traditionally an American because the program is very popular in the United States and that country provides a large share of the donations to UNICEF.

The popularity of the program is reflected in the support it gets at all levels. Few member nations want to be the ones to stand in the way of UNICEF's continued success, and so when UNICEF needs money or approval for projects, member nations put aside their differences and work multinationally in the interests of the fund and the children. This is not always the case with other organizations, where political power plays can influence outcomes. When UNICEF needed to transform and modernize its headquarters, negotiations with its member states to acquire a loan to buy the land, including the garage adjacent to the old building, were not subjected to a hard and tiring fundraising effort, nor were the negotiations subject to much politicizing, as has been the case in other United Nations Organizations. I was the head of the Admin and Finance Committee in the Board at the time and later became the vice-president of the board, and while the task was not easy, it was also not impossible: the loan was secured and a new building was erected, and from the 1980s onward UNICEF continued their work in a healthy, convenient environment.

UNICEF's mandate to care for the health and welfare of mothers and children in developing countries takes into consideration the limited means at the disposal of those countries. Two examples demonstrate that. Diarrhea kills many children, so UNICEF invented a cheap, simple solution in the form of a plastic bag containing a mixture of sugar and salt to fight that disease in an effective way. To avoid diarrhea, drinking water must be purified, especially in rural villages, and to do this within the limited means of people living there, UNICEF designed a simple manual pump that can easily be secured. One head of the Admin and Finance Committee witnessed and experienced the value of these two programs the hard way when he himself got the disease through contaminated water and carried his diarrhea through the duration of the mission and the break he took after that. However, it was a lesson well learned about some of the acute problems facing the developing countries. The lesson learned would not have been possible sitting comfortably in the organization's headquarters in New York City or lounging in a hotel while on mission.

The story of development does not end by raising a child (UNICEF) and educating him (UNESCO); rather, it is the beginning. Other specialized agencies come in to supplement UNESCO's work and complete the journey of growing up: The World Health Organization (WHO) cares for children's health until they reach adulthood; the Food and Agriculture Organization (FAO) makes sure that they eat well; the International Labour Organization (ILO) helps them to earn a living; and with the Bretton Woods Institutions, the Big Five, the originals of the agencies since the creation of the United Nations System, take on the essential task of financing operations. The story is fine-tuned by an array of agencies, funds, and programs that complement the work of the Big Five. Therefore, it is true, as it has often been said, that if the United Nations did not exist, it would need to be created. Experience has proved this over and over.

The UN Oil-for-Food Program

As a result of the Iraqi occupation of Kuwait in 1990 and following the end of the first Gulf War, the United Nations imposed sanctions on the Iraqi regime. However, to allow people access to food and other necessities, the United Nations initiated the Oil-For-Food Program in 1996 to permit the Iraqi Government to secure these essentials. Unfortunately, the program was mismanaged and badly handled through kickbacks, surcharges, and smuggling undertaken by some Iraqi officials, as well as some United Nations officers close to the program or who were working for it.

In 2004, a United Nations Independent Inquiry Committee headed by former US Federal Reserve Chairman Paul Volcker took a close look into the management of the program. In one of its initial reports, the commission blamed the program management because it "operated in an ineffective, wasteful and unsatisfactory manner."[2] The United Nations was supposed to control the process of selling Iraqi oil in exchange for food as well as control the procurement of goods bought by the oil sale. However, this was done in a loose manner, giving the Iraqi regime the freedom of choosing both the oil sale and the goods procurement. The oil sale mishandling was done by a scheme of vouchers that were given to friendly governments, companies, and individuals in return for their influence or services for the benefit of the regime. The vouchers were priced at a lower rate for the beneficiaries so that when they sold them at the market price, they netted some profit. All this was done in violation of the program's rules and methods, the result of clear corruption. Of course, the money from the kickbacks was not used to buy food and necessities for the Iraqi people.

The actors in this corruption case included presidents, directors, chairmen, officials, businessmen, military officials, and civilians, many of whom are not held accountable for their actions. When the scheme developed into a scandal, nearly all concerned either simply resigned or disappeared, and all denied any wrongdoing. Their actions are reminiscent of the violent challenges in football, in which one player pushes a player from the opposing team, sending him writhing on the ground in pain while the one who pushed him raises both hands to indicate that he did nothing wrong. All this is watched by the referee and filmed on camera. If the referee punishes the challenger, he rushes to the referee, shouting and protesting. What a change from the sportsmanship of yesterday's football.

The United Nations Security Council did nothing about the scandal, nor did the General Assembly or the ICJ. When money is mishandled, it is corruption; when the amount is bigger, it is Corruption; and when it is huge, it is CORRUPTION. In the Oil-For-Food case, billions of dollars exchanged hands, including $1.7 billion through kickbacks and surcharges and $10.9 billion through illegal *oil* smuggling.[3]

If there is a lesson to be learned from the Oil-for-Food case, it is that money corrupts, which is a phenomenon that we have witnessed throughout ancient as well as modern history. When one deals with millions or billions of dollars, the temptation for corruption is there. However, the real calamity lies in depriving those who were supposed to benefit from this money—the Iraqi people, for whom the money should have provided the funding to nourish them and treat their sick. It is a crime to play with the money destined for them. If the main organs in the United Nations did not address the case in a satisfactory manner, what guarantee do we have that it will not happen again? The Oil-for-Food scandal also unearthed a methodology of secrecy that seemed to be adopted by the Secretariat of the United Nations. Do we have to wait for another case like this to address the wrongdoing that may exist in the organization's methods of operations?

We have come across material relating to the establishment and the main organs of the United Nations and will touch upon the financing of the organization, but we already have a negative case dealing with mismanaging financial appropriations. Just as other authors and writers have done, we have referred to the size, material, and staff of the United Nations Organization and to the colossal budgets that this entails. The extraordinary amount of money budgeted for the execution of programs makes fertile ground for overlapping and repetition, and if projects are not handled with efficiency and proper oversight, it can eventually lead to corruption. One will always hope for better performance, considering the resources that are at the disposal of the United Nations. Otherwise, how can one explain that the organization has been sidelined all these years from the main events happening in the same world that the United Nations is mandated to keep the peace in for the purpose of developing that world? There are many examples, but COVID-19 and the mishandling of the international response is a recent one.

The case of the Oil-for-Food scandal sends a clear signal for why it is necessary to undertake major United Nations reforms that go deep to the roots of the way the organization is functioning. Nothing short of major reform will stop similar cases from surfacing in the future.

One would think that awareness and preparedness on the part of the United Nations System for caring and developing a life of happiness for human beings is obvious. Alas, much as we wish that noble target to be true, reality tells us otherwise. Consider calamities like global warming, various wars and disputes around the world, the many multinational companies and corporations that enslave employees to reap profits for their stakeholders, deforestation, and the extermination of wildlife. To a major extent, the human beings who the United Nations sets out to develop are themselves responsible for the damage inflicted on the planet. The decision makers in the System make development difficult through their ongoing political rivalries and by putting their national interests ahead of development. It is both comical and tragic to witness these rivalries manifest when it comes to the United Nations' response to crisis management, but it is hard to swallow such struggles when the matter is financing a developmental project like constructing a dam, building an electricity grid, financing a habitat, or initiating a horticulture project. These are highly technical, beneficial projects that will improve the quality of life for human beings. How can we allow these matters to be the subject of controversy?

If decision makers in the United Nations politicize such decisions, that also sets a precedent for those who are deprived of humanity. It is high time to subject the assistance given by the United Nations to its member states to thorough revision so that we can change the present situation and focus on the need of making the lives of the citizens in developing countries better.

Notes

1 "Key Data on UNESCO Staff," Management Support and Coordination Unit (HRM/MSC), January 2022, rev. April 6, 2022, https://web.archive.org/web/20240306173121/https://en.unesco.org/sites/default/files/key_data_jan_2022_0.pdf.

2 Sharon Otterman, "IRAQ: Oil for Food Scandal," Council on Foreign Relations, https://www.cfr.org/backgrounder/iraq-oil-food-scandal.

3 Otterman, "IRAQ: Oil for Food Scandal."

4

Performance of the United Nations Crisis Response

The crisis response of the United Nations System to many disputes, conflicts, and struggles has developed into a crisis of its own. Scores of conflicts in which the System has tried to initiate solutions that will put an end to the conflicts have not come close to final and sure settlements, much to the disappointment of the United Nations. Consequently, many of these conflicts are in a stalemate. Periodic attempts to reactivate plans for ending them only arrive at another impasse. Some of the disputes became dormant without a solution, and nobody asks about them anymore. This situation became a trademark for the United Nations crisis management, tarnishing the organization's reputation for a reason not entirely of its own making. One could even venture to say that in the blame game, the responsibility for this unfavorable situation falls first and foremost on nationalism coming from the member states rather than on the United Nations System, which represents multilateralism. One should bear in mind that the United Nations has no army, only an observation force to enforce its decisions in peacekeeping, and it is a matter of principle not to have an army because the organization advocates peaceful means in solving disputes. On the other hand, military forces are sometimes used in member states to settle conflicts. This is an old, contradictory situation that will not be advantageous to peacekeeping.

In the early stages of a dispute, the United Nations, represented by the Security Council, will take up the matter so that the dispute does not transform into a threat to international peace and security. Efforts within the council make it a priority to settle the dispute by peaceful means, according to Chapter Six of the charter. When belligerents fail to restore peace, the council passes to a second stage relating to the use of force to arrive at the settlement, as stipulated in Chapter Seven of the charter. An important element here is that the forces used by the United Nations to enforce its decisions come from the member states by obligation and that the application of those decisions is mandatory for all members of the organization. One can justifiably ask whether the deployment of national forces from member states for keeping international peace and security will or will not have a national agenda behind it. More concretely, some member states will advocate peaceful settlement of a dispute but secretly sell arms to one of the belligerents for economic purposes, thereby directly or indirectly prolonging the dispute. This results in an adverse effect on international peace and security, as witnessed today by many disputes and conflicts that have endured for a long time in Mali, Western Sahara, Cyprus, Palestine, Congo, Azerbaijan, and the remnants of the Balkans.

A relatively rare success story is of the international cooperation, through the United Nations, in the liberation of Kuwait from Iraqi occupation in 1991. Perhaps more typical is the case of war-torn Syria, with respect to which one permanent member (Russia) has vetoed seven peace resolutions between 2011 and 2022. In the effort of maintaining international peace and security, the United Nations will always confront the hurdle that anything between the boundaries of member states falls under the category of sovereignty, although the jurisdiction of the United Nations covers all member countries, and so those countries are bound to apply the organization's decisions, especially the ones that are taken under Chapter Seven. Since the United Nations has no permanent force of its own, there is a paradox here in that all applications of its decisions will be marred by national tendencies and policies. This paradox is aggravated by the right of veto and permanent membership that the Permanent Five have in the Security Council. Unless major reform occurs to remedy this unfavorable situation, peacekeeping attempts by the United Nations will be handicapped, and it is no wonder that regional conflicts around the world endure.

One should not discredit the sale of armaments that add fuel to the fire. Consider and compare the difference between the sale of a box of Kleenex and a military aircraft, one to advocate cleanliness and the other to kill people and destroy property. The difference in profit between selling a box of Kleenex and an aircraft is colossal, even though it's all trade. Unless a follow-up export team is formed by the United Nations to investigate, analyze, and contribute to the solutions, the trouble spots will continue to exist, negatively compromising the United Nations' effort to secure effective and permanent ways to eradicate threats to international peace and security caused by those trouble spots.

Liberation of Kuwait (A United Nations Success Story)

Iraq and Kuwait are two adjacent Arab countries with a long history of good neighborly relations. Both countries are oil producers with rich reserves. Iraq is also a fertile agricultural country thanks to its two rivers, the Tigris and the Euphrates. Unfortunately, Iraq in its modern history has had unstable regimes marked by several *coups d'etat*. Furthermore, a change in regime in neighboring Iran during the 1980s saw a war between the two countries. Financing a modern war costs much more than embarking on developmental projects; however, a country at war cannot afford development. During the war with Iran, Iraq turned to its brotherly country immediately to the south, Kuwait, for financial assistance. The latter responded positively by lending Iraq the necessary capital. With time and continued military engagements, the sum of the debt kept increasing, and by the time that a ceasefire was declared between Iraq and Iran, the former owed Kuwait $11 billion. Right after the war, Kuwait requested repayment of the debt. Iraq, which at the time had the fourth-strongest military in the region, refused to succumb to Kuwaiti claims in such a difficult conflict atmosphere. Other neighboring countries, particularly Saudi Arabia, stepped in to mediate between Iraq and Kuwait in an effort to find a solution for the debt. Saudi Arabia's King Fahad even offered his financial help to decrease the sum that Iraq should pay to Kuwait. However, they could not find a solution, and a stormy meeting between the two parties in Geneva in January 1991 did not accomplish much. What aggravated the dispute is that Iraq also accused Kuwait of drilling for oil in its territorial waters.

Another obstacle to peace was that Iraq claimed that Kuwait was part of its territory that had been sliced out as an independent state by the colonialists. On the day it was granted independence from Britain, June 19, 1961, the Iraqi leader, Abdulkarim Kassim, said that Kuwait would have to ask for Arab help to safeguard its independence. Egypt responded and sent its troops to be stationed along the Kuwaiti borders with Iraq. Did Iraq's Saddam Hussein have the invasion of Kuwait in mind when he accepted a ceasefire with Iran and as he considered what to do with a strong Iraqi Army that seemingly did well against Iran?

The possibilities seem enticing: effacing the debt, stopping the illegal drilling, and unearthing the claim to Kuwait. Consider too the marked difference in size and capacities of the two countries and the possibility of a coup by the Iraqi Army. Iraq tested the waters by suggesting that Kuwait merge with Iraq. At a meeting with Saddam Hussein in Baghdad, the US ambassador, April Glaspie, indicated that the United States considered Iraqi policy toward Kuwait as an Iraqi internal affair. The cold American attitude toward burning issues between Iraq and Kuwait was mistaken by the Iraqi authorities as indifference toward any measures that Iraq undertook concerning its southern neighbor.

Glaspie's remarks, combined with the other considerations, constituted a strong motive for marching in and occupying its southern neighbor, which is exactly what happened on August 2, 1990. The occupation of Kuwait by Iraq came as a surprise, judging by the almost unanimous condemnation from the international community and by the large coalition of thirty-six countries that sent their armies to end that occupation under the leadership of the United States of America. From the immediate steps that Iraq took in Kuwait regarding the country's archives, population registration, and demography, it was evident that Iraq intended to completely annex Kuwait. Considering the big difference between the two countries, many people, including Kuwaitis, were rather demoralized, giving up hope that their country would ever be independent again.

As it should be, the United Nations was associated with the calamity of an occupation from the beginning till the end. The United Nations applied all the rules in the book to end it, including the entirety of Chapter Six in the charter dealing with Pacific Settlement of Disputes, and, when that was not enough, it turned to Chapter Seven, which is related to the use of force to terminate aggression. The Security Council approved more than ten binding resolutions to end the occupation by force through an international coalition. The problem was an absence of any balance between those resolutions and the Iraqi action because Iraq simply ignored them and did not pay any attention to the views of the international community. Iraq just went ahead and occupied Kuwait.

Iraq expected the liberation military attack to come from the sea through the Gulf. Instead, coalition forces went westward, deep into Saudi Arabia, then turned north and finally eastward to Kuwait. They met with no resistance from the Iraqi Army, which simply headed north to its borders and returned home almost intact. Not for long, though, because twelve years later, in 2003, Iraq was almost destroyed by the American forces in an attack that was not sanctioned by the United Nations—but that is another drama and story. It is perhaps cynical to ask whether the liberation of Kuwait would have happened if the country was not oil-rich, but regardless of the answer, the liberation of Kuwait from the Iraqi occupation is a true success story for the United Nations and by the United Nations. It gave the organization a chance to legally play by the book and apply all the steps in its charter. The UN did a good job of it, keeping international peace and security in the world and thus fulfilling the mandate of its charter.

This success story shows why it does not work to use national methods to solve international problems. Success in Kuwait was attained when the international rules of engagement were adhered to, in that the United Nations treated the problem under its auspices, and delegates of member states acted as international representatives of the organization and not on behalf of their governments seeking national interests. This is unlike the situation with many enduring conflicts, where a key reason for not solving them all this time is the conflicting interests of member states, including those who serve on the Security Council. Unless a dispute is treated by the United Nations and through the United Nations, including delegates and staff acting in an international (i.e., non-nationalist) manner, the United Nations will not be able to solve it. Scores of disputes around the world drag on without any conclusive solutions to them because a solution suggested by one country goes against the interests of another, and unless that attitude of nationalism is transformed into an attitude that serves only the interests of the United Nations, which is the sum total of national interests combined in an international spirit, the United Nations will not be able to end disputes.

Civil War in Kosovo

Kosovo is an autonomous region within the former Yugoslavia with an Albanian majority. In 1998, an armed conflict erupted between the troops of the Federal Republic of Yugoslavia, which tried to keep Kosovo within the federation, and the Kosovo Liberation Army (KLA), which attempted to keep the enclave separate from Yugoslavia. The war lasted nearly a year and a half, with the KLA gaining the support of NATO air power. The Treaty of Kumanovo ended the war through the intervention of the United Nations, according to Security Council Resolutions 1239 and 1244, whereby the United Nations was mandated to manage Kosovo by an international administration.[1] The main cause of the war was the continuous persecution of the Kosovo Albanians by the Serbs, which led to the formation of the KLA in the early 1990s. When the subject was brought to the United Nations Security Council in 1999, it was difficult to address it from a political angle with the aim of finding a solution because the former Yugoslavia, supported by the Eastern Bloc countries, objected to that tendency while the West supported it. That made the negotiations for a settlement difficult. In the end, the preamble of the draft resolution expressed the wish of the council to arrive at a political solution for the conflict, while the working paragraphs concentrated on the economic and humanitarian aspects. Consequently, the unanimously approved Resolution 1239 (1999) came to light.

The Security Council was rather timid in its approach to the problem of Kosovo in that it dealt with it from the humanitarian angle, considering the flow of refugees and displaced persons from the enclave to other parts of Yugoslavia. They took this approach because the Eastern Bloc objected to any condemnations and measures that the council might take against the Serbs while the West was ready to approve them. The only reference to any political solution was made in paragraph 6 of Resolution 1239 (1999), in which the Security Council notes that "the humanitarian situation will continue to deteriorate in the absence of a political solution."[2] Putting the political content in the preamble and the humanitarian aspects in the working paragraphs was a way to dilute the objections.

Come June 10, 1999, the Security Council took up the problem of Kosovo again, and this time it was adamant to discuss it from all angles, be it political, military, or humanitarian. The council stressed the need to stop Serbian violence against Muslims, to ensure the autonomy of Kosovo, and to allow the United Nations to establish an international administration to run the affairs in the enclave. The Security Council ended its deliberations by approving and adopting Resolution 1244 (1999).[3] This time the council was unanimous in its approach, and that gave it the chance to deal with the matter in detail and to take comprehensive action. As time went by, the world saw the disintegration of the Federal Republic of Yugoslavia into several independent states.

The Kosovo War is only an episode in several ethnic conflicts that took place in the Federal Republic of Yugoslavia and that caused the systemic disintegration of the Republic into several independent states. In a way, it is like the situations in Rwanda and the Democratic Republic of Congo (DRC), where ethnic tensions were not ironed out in a peaceful way. Consider, for example, the massacre of Srebrenica, where as many as 8,000 Muslims were slaughtered by the Bosnian Serbs in the United Nations haven. Although a United Nations Dutch infantry battalion was present, it failed to intervene, overwhelmed by superior firepower and lack of air support. Subsequent investigations of the Srebrenica massacre by the United Nations itself concluded that, "Through error, misjudgement and an inability to recognize the scope of the evil confronting us, we failed to do our part to help save the people of Srebrenica from the Serb campaign of mass murder."[4] Other analyses have placed the blame on an ineffective chain of command. Although national forces deployed as peacekeepers are supposed to be under the exclusive command and control of the United Nations, Dutch field commanders in Kosovo were in regular communication with senior commanders in The Hague, as well as senior UN commanders.[5] The ineffective chain of command that David Bosco identifies as a cause for the failure of the mission may highlight a more general difficulty with peacekeeping missions, namely, the inevitable tension between the objectives of the UN mission and the tolerance for risk of the countries providing troops.

Civil War in Congo

This case study is related to what is known today as the DRC (capital: Kinshasa), formerly a colony known as the Belgian Congo. It should not be confused with the Republic of Congo (capital: Brazzaville), which was part of the French Congo during colonial times and which lies adjacent to the DRC.

The crisis began in 1960, just after the DRC gained its independence from Belgium on June 30, 1960. Internal strife, fueled by the rivalry within the Cold War between the West under the leadership of the United States of America and the East under the banner of the Soviet Union, resulted in secessionist attempts by certain local leaders. The ensuing civil wars lasted five years and resulted in a toll of nearly 100,000 victims. The conflict ended when Colonel Joseph-Desire Mobutu gained control of the whole country. During his rule, the country was renamed Zaïre in 1971 and continued for thirty-two years in an authoritarian way until he was deposed in 1997.

At the end of the Belgian colonial rule, the resource-rich country was ill-prepared for independence. Three fundamental elements were not dealt with peacefully or in a satisfactory way: federalism, tribalism, and ethnic nationalism. Disagreement on these matters partly explains the civil wars, disputes, and conflicts that erupted immediately after independence, starting with the violence that followed the secession of the Katanga region in the south and South Kasai in the north. This dangerous situation prompted the United Nations secretary-general, Dag Hammarskjöld, to send peacekeeping troops to the country after securing the agreement of the Security Council. It is noteworthy that the United Nations soldiers came from Sweden, Hammarskjöld's country of origin. However, while the secretary-general sent troops to the region, he refused to aid the government in its efforts to end the two secession attempts. This prompted the prime minister of the DRC, Patrice Lumumba, to demand the help of the Soviet Union, thus causing a rift between him and President Joseph Kasa-Vubu. As their disagreement intensified, Lumumba and Kasa-Vubu both ordered the army chief of staff, Joseph-Desire Mobutu (Mobutu Sese Seko), to kill their opponent. Instead, Mobutu ended the stalemate by mounting a *coup d'état* that sent the Soviets home, executed Lumumba, and took total control of the government. The supporters of the executed prime minister in the east of the country subsequently mounted a mutiny but were defeated by government troops. After the mysterious death of Secretary-General Hammarskjöld in a plane crash on September 18, 1961, the United Nations troops took a more active role, which proved to be decisive in ending the secession of Katanga and South Kasai in 1963. Soon after that, reconciliatory efforts were undertaken to form an interim administration.

The Katangese leader, Moïse Tshombe, was asked to head that administration. At the same time, certain militants calling themselves the Simbas tried to control parts of the country but were defeated, and government troops recovered the territories. Elections were finally held in 1965, but peace and stability did not reign because a stalemate ensued between Tshombe and President Kasa-Vubu; this ultimately prompted Mobutu, by then a major-general, to mount his second *coup d'état*, taking full control of the country for a long period that ended in 1977.

As if what happened in the DRC by way of mutinies, violence, disputes, and conflicts that resulted in 100,000 casualties was not enough, the country has suffered, and still suffers, from the remnant of the genocide that took place in neighboring Rwanda to the east of the DRC. Before the genocide happened, the United Nations sent an observation mission headed by the Canadian General Romeo Dallaire to supervise the agreement between the Hutu government and the Tutsi Rwandan Patriotic Front. The general knew of the planned genocide and informed the United Nations headquarters in New York but was advised not to act. This cold reaction of the United Nations kept the general silent during the genocide, but when it was over, he insinuated that with a stronger United Nations mandate in Rwanda and an extra 5,000 troops in addition to his soldiers, he could have saved "hundreds of thousands" of lives. Obviously, some influential powers in the Security Council did not see eye to eye with him.

The genocide started on April 6, 1994, as a result of the arch-rivalry between the majority Hutu and the minority Tutsi tribes. The Hutu leaders had planned to completely wipe out the Tutsis, and during April and May 1994, which marked the most intense days of the genocide, between 800,000 and one million Tutsis lost their lives. Later, the tables turned when the Tutsis came to power and started what they called "revenge killings," during which

100,000 Hutus were killed. To escape these retaliatory attacks, an estimated two million Hutus fled the country to the neighboring DRC. Militants among the refugees started killing Tutsis in the DRC, in response to which the Tutsi government in Kigali sent troops to the DRC, thus adding to the violence in an already unstable country. These tensions continue to flare up sporadically to this day.

The situation in the DRC was complicated even more when, in late 2013, refugees from the neighboring Central African Republic began to pour into the country after renewed violence followed the failed elections in their country. The instability in the DRC and its neighboring countries is not helped by the fact that, behind the scenes, Eastern and Western international governments and corporations compete for the country's ample and varied resources. Every time the United Nations Security Council reviews the United Nations Operation in Congo (ONUC), some members of the council touch upon the deteriorating situation in the country; however, no one has suggested solutions that might provide the DRC with the required peace and security necessary for the development of its ample resources. Instead of ironing out the problems related to federalism, tribalism, and ethnic nationalism, the colonial powers have nurtured the conflicts in ways that allow their companies to get the lion's share of profits from the development of the country's rich resources.

COVID-19 (as a Crisis Response)

Contrary to expectations, the United Nations System was slow in reacting to the spread of the pandemic. The World Health Organization (WHO), which is part of the System, announced the spread of the virus earlier, but rather than leading to international cooperation and to containment of the virus, it instead exposed the technical agency to the political row among the world's influential states, thus politicizing the pandemic. WHO could talk about and deal with the medical aspects of the virus, but it is not mandated to handle the political implications, which fall under the business of the United Nations General Assembly and the Security Council. As soon as the world knew about the pandemic, differences of opinion arose between the United States of America and China, where the virus originated, about what to call the virus and how to deal with it, which in turn led to another rift between the United States and the WHO. This unsatisfactory situation caused unwarranted delays in the General Assembly and Security Council's ability to react swiftly, and this ultimately resulted in a lukewarm response to the pandemic. More than three months passed after the WHO's declaration about COVID-19 before the General Assembly and the Security Council made a move to deliberate the matter; in the meanwhile, the virus was ravaging communities around the world, infecting and killing people and turning the lives of survivors upside down.

Once it had been decided that the political organs of the United Nations System should break the silence and do something to address this dangerous world situation, the General Assembly met to discuss the matter and subsequently issued resolution A/RES/74/270 of April 2, 2020.[6] In that resolution, the Assembly pointed out the danger and threat to human life that the pandemic held and outlined the far-reaching, devastating negative effect it would have on the world economy. In praising the good work that individuals and organizations were doing around the globe, it emphasized the importance of a concerted group effort by all concerned, since all individuals and countries were affected by the virus. Instead of a united effort, everybody and every country or group dealt with the virus in its own way and developed their own vaccine rather than coordinating their efforts. As a result, confusion reigned, and that increased the number of cases and deaths. It also confirmed how nationalist tendencies take precedence over multinationalism.

The General Assembly's resolution, approved unanimously, was comprehensive, straightforward, and clear enough to make people of the world aware of the danger posed by the pandemic. However, the General Assembly has no power to enforce the application of its resolutions on member states—that power rests with the Security Council. In this instance, the Security Council may have felt embarrassed that the WHO was energetically working on the matter and the General Assembly had so pointedly addressed it while the council had not yet made a move. Despite that delay, and considering the difference of opinion regarding how to handle COVID-19 among some influential members of the council, it nonetheless took up the subject in an indirect way, from the angle of the threat of the pandemic to international peace and security, which lies at the heart and soul of the Security Council's mandate. However, Chapter Six of the charter outlines the scope of the disputes that fall under the Security Council's area of responsibility, while Chapter Seven stipulates the steps for using force to face the specified conflicts when peaceful means fail. In the case of the pandemic, there was no fighting, and the Council's Resolution 2532 of 2020 approved after its deliberation on COVID-19, made no reference to the use of force under Chapter Seven.[7] The dangers and threats posed by the virus are more overbearing and more widespread than armed disputes. COVID-19 nearly paralyzed all aspects of living, ruined economies, shattered social lives, and caused two and a half million deaths with 110 million cases worldwide.

How the United Nations System fared in dealing with this international calamity remains open to question. The least that can be said is that the United Nations' handling of the pandemic was below expectations. Efforts to combat and contain the virus, nationally or internationally, were uncoordinated and dispersed and characterized by rivalry and marked by differences when they should have been complementary. The United Nations shares the blame for the failed response to the pandemic but should not bear all the blame. The organization and its ability to respond effectively fell victim to the continuing rivalry among some influential members of the Security Council, especially the veto holders.

The Russian Invasion of Ukraine and the United Nations' Timid Response

The United Nations' single most important mandates are to keep peace in the world and to assist in developing and ameliorating the lives of its inhabitants. It is the only organization that is entrusted with this comprehensive and far-reaching task. It makes sense, then, to assume that if a crisis arises among member countries, it is the responsibility of the United Nations to handle that crisis. It must try to find a solution to the crisis, thus keeping the peace, and the charter should provide the foundation on which it can build its response. The charter of the organization assumes that the United Nations and all its organs work to see that this mandate is adhered to and enforced, but what happens when the charter itself doesn't cover the scope of a crisis, as happened with COVID-19?

At the time of writing, a new crisis is underway and is summarized in the Russian fear that Ukraine, which is adjacent to it with common borders, might constitute a security danger if it joins the Western EU and NATO. Hence, a former member of the defunct Soviet Union will join the West side in the everlasting struggle between the East and the West. If this happens, the Russians think, the regime in Kyiv, the capital of Ukraine, will cease to be "friendly" to them like the majority of the neighboring countries, former parts of the Soviet Union, like Belarus, for example. After the Cold War, people thought that the rivalry between the East and the West was over. The present crisis proves the contrary. Russia has already annexed Ukraine's island of Crimea. This explains in part the Ukrainian policy leaning toward the West. It will be hard to believe that the Russians, by threatening Ukraine, will not also annex more or the rest of that country. The memory of Kuwait being annexed by Iraq in 1990 is still vivid. In that case, the whole world was unified in opposing that annexation, liberating Kuwait in 1991. Things stand differently now. One tends to believe that if Russia occupies the whole of Ukraine, the worst scenario will be to "establish" a "friendly" regime in it and then get out. In any case, the crisis is at its height, making the outcome unpredictable at this point in time.

The main concern is that the crisis is part and parcel of the responsibility of the United Nations based on the articles of Chapter Six of its charter, which relates to the Pacific Settlement of Disputes. This is what is needed to deal with the present situation that the crisis is passing through. When the crisis transformed into an armed conflict, then articles of Chapter Seven would apply. At the moment, negotiations to defuse the situation are at their summit between the parties concerned, but where is the United Nations, and where is its secretary-general in all this? At the same time, the Russian military attacks on Ukraine are going on unabated, together with Ukrainian repulses aided by the West. The news media did not report any consultation with the council nor its officials, except for a fruitless meeting with President Putin and a visit by the secretary-general to Kyiv for humanitarian purposes. Deliberations took place in the United Nations organ mandated to resolve the crisis, namely the Security Council, but with no practical outcome because the veto casting threat by the Russians. Furthermore, nobody seems to be aware of any secret contacts with the United Nations or its secretary-general. The organization and its top officials were totally ignored by the belligerents, something that should not be passed in silence. Pushing the United Nations aside in responding to an international crisis is harmful and unproductive to the crisis outcome. Solving them should not be handled nationally but multilaterally by the only organization concerned, and that is the United Nations. If the latter is sidelined intentionally or otherwise, the United Nations should, through its secretary-general, speak to the media protesting in a diplomatic way. He will have the right in what he says. Furthermore, the International Security Council will be on the right side if it meets to discuss the Russian-Ukraine crisis, taking at the end the appropriate resolution(s) that it sees fit to resolve that crisis. If that does not happen, the letters of support for the United Nations that the world leaders write and the speeches that they deliver in this regard and on various occasions will be meaningless when it comes to international peace and security. It would seem irrelevant to blame the United Nations for not responding to a crisis when it is prevented from handling what falls within its jurisdiction.

As the build-up to the Russian-Ukraine crisis unfolded, reaching its climax through massive troops of the former at the latter's border, the Security Council met several times to take up the matter. It was through the exercise of lip service on the part of the council. The crisis amounts to a threat to the independence of a small country compared to a neighboring threatening world power. The timid approach of the council to the crisis could not be otherwise for reasons that have been referred to and analyzed in this book.

The council's deliberations resulted in a draft resolution presented by the United States on behalf of the West, only to be vetoed by the Russian Federation. Bad luck has it for Ukraine that its belligerent, Russia, is a permanent member of the council that possesses a veto power. Therefore, it can block anything coming out of the council that does not meet its approval. It is rather odd to see the United Nations powerless in trying to diffuse a crisis, as it is expected to, for a fault not of its own, but due to a shortcoming in its original structure. It is noteworthy to know that, regarding the crisis, the application of Chapter Six of the charter was done, but outside the realm of the Security Council. This was done by various consultations among world leaders with the Russian and Ukrainian presidents in attempts to alleviate the situation so that the conflict does not transform into an armed one. However, all this was done outside the Security Council and obviously without its knowledge. In any case, all the efforts failed to resolve the problem. It is not surprising because the United Nations' role was ignored. Secondly, and outside the United Nations, the crisis was mishandled by advocating justifications that were not convincing. In the end, it was power politics that saw recourse to force as the only way.

When Russia attacked Ukraine on Thursday, February 22, 2022, in an unexpected way, at least to the general public, it was quite surprising to see a major world power attacking a relatively small country. It was time to move from Chapter Six of the charter to Chapter Seven (Action with Respect to Threats to the Aggression). Only now the United Nations was involved in a major way. The United States of America tabled a draft resolution calling for an end to the Russian aggression. It was a bit late, though, but in the right direction just the same. The expectation of the result of the voting on the draft resolution was more than real because Russia vetoed it, as Russia is part of the P5 Group. As expected, yet again, the United Nations was powerless in trying to make a positive response to the crisis.

Additionally, the crisis was not Ukrainian per se but fell within the rivalry between East and West under the leadership of the Russian Federation and the United States of America. The crisis was aggravated by the transformation of the regime in Kyiv from a socialist to a capitalist political and economic system. For the Russian Federation, this represents a security threat at its doorstep. Therefore, this situation turned the crisis from a bilateral into a multilateral explosive situation. One would think of the fate of small and medium-sized ... fall in the circle of world power politics with rivalry among ... Those countries cannot even seek refuge in the United ... powers control the organization as well, either by the ... the possession of the veto power or both.

... perceptive article, written by Simon Tisdall, calls ... by the organization in the invasion.[8] This is ... ian veto in the Security Council making the ... the General Assembly as a base for approval.

The majority against the invasion is there. This is a suggestion that is debated in the UN circles in attempts to reform the organization. Here is a political and live occasion to apply it.

Tisdall is using the invasion also to dig deep into an ongoing exercise to revitalize the UN so that it can play a more productive role in world affairs. He calls on the present secretary-general of the organization, António Guterres, to call for a fundamental conference similar to that held in 1945 that established the UN. The aim is to relaunch the UN institutionally and organizationally "in ways that reflect the global power balances and priorities of the 21st century." Using the invasion in such a way is, to our mind, both a golden and detrimental opportunity for the benefit of both Ukraine and the UN. If the UN fails to use it in order to play a better role in a world crisis like this one, the writer rightly says that it "may be catastrophic for all."[9]

International Law and the Expected Role of the UN in the Gaza Crisis Response

On October 7, 2023, the military wing of Hamas launched a surprise attack on Israeli military and civilian targets. The unusual operation took the Israeli defense forces completely off guard and provoked a fierce reaction on targets in the Gaza Strip. Besides continuous aerial bombardments, the Israeli defense forces continue to enforce a near-total ban on humanitarian relief for Gaza's civilian population, leaving its residents without necessities like food, fresh water, and medical supplies. The provocation of Hamas caused the scope, scale, and severity of the Israeli response and its apparent disregard for the welfare of Gazan civilians. While world public opinion was very intense, the global crisis response was tentative, at best.

The purpose of this analysis is to review what international law says ab
the Palestinian–Israeli conflict, to examine the expected and appropri
of the United Nations in the context of international law, and to e
the United Nations' performance of that role. What happened in
viewed as yet another example of unsatisfactory crisis respons
Nations.

At the United Nations, the latest chapter of the Palestinian–Israeli conflict was taken very seriously due to the dehumanizing character of the crisis. As human casualties, including noncombatants, continued to rise, Secretary-General António Guterres and his associates flew to the region on October 19, 2023, to address the humanitarian dimensions of the crisis and visited the Rafah crossing between Gaza and Egypt on October 20. The goal of this mission was to ensure that desperately needed humanitarian assistance could pass across the border to the besieged enclave of more than two million people. That objective required hard negotiations with the concerned authorities and resulted in an agreement to reopen the border. Trucks carrying humanitarian assistance were finally permitted to cross into Gaza on October 20, although not in sufficient numbers to address the extent of human need.

Having succeeded, at least provisionally, in addressing the immediate humanitarian dimensions of the Hamas–Israeli conflict, the secretary-general returned to New York to participate in discussions of the political aspects of the crisis in the Security Council. When his turn came to speak, Secretary-General Guterres stated that what Hamas militants did on October 7 had a historical context and did not come from a vacuum. This view was contrary to the official Israeli position, which considered the Hamas attack as an isolated and altogether unprovoked event.

Far from seeking to justify the actions of Hamas, the secretary-general reminded the council that these actions should not be viewed as the beginning of a conflict but rather as the latest in a decades-long one. He was surely referring to the historical roots of the problem, namely the direct Israeli occupation of Gaza in 1948, which in 2005 morphed into a siege, turning the region into something akin to apartheid or an open prison. Israel has maintained strict control over Gaza's air and maritime space since then, as well as six of Gaza's seven land crossings, leaving the residents of Gaza completely dependent on Israel for water, electricity, and telecommunications. Even the official population registry of Gaza is subject to Israel's control.

When the Security Council took up the matter, and as expected, at least by the world's general opinion, disappointment was the order of the day. The discussion got precisely nowhere despite the grave humanitarian dimensions of the crisis. When the time finally came to make a decision, the Security

Council was unable to take any action, owing to sharp differences in opinion among its members. Under the circumstances, the only draft resolution that could be tabled addressed the humanitarian, rather than the political and military, aspects of the crisis. Specifically, the resolution (S/2023/773) called for a "humanitarian pause" in the fighting to allow for aid to reach the residents of Gaza.[10] Even this relatively mild measure was vetoed by one of the permanent members, for failing to include an amendment with an explicit political connotation.

Recurring examples of the inability of the "closed club" of fifteen Security Council members to do productive work have delayed finding resolutions for many conflicts, not only in the case of the Gaza crisis or, indeed, the Arab–Israeli conflict as a whole. As a customary procedure, when the Security Council fails to reach a conclusive agreement on matters, urgent issues can be taken to the General Assembly. In the General Assembly, they are discussed under a catch-all agenda item known as "United for Peace." One can assume, perhaps, that justice is more likely to be served at the General Assembly than the Security Council, if only because no single country has the authority to veto a measure approved by the entire body. However, while the deliberations of the General Assembly take place in a more democratic atmosphere, in which all UN members are represented and are free to openly express their opinions, the resolutions of the General Assembly are not binding. Without the concurrence of the Security Council and the support of the Permanent Five, any resolution from the General Assembly remains symbolic.

The power of the veto can even be used to defy international law so long as its wielder believes itself to be unaccountable to world opinion. It is, perhaps, illustrative that France and the UK have not used the veto since 1989, while the United States, Russia, and, to a lesser extent, China, continue to do so regularly. Insofar as the UN Charter is itself a foundational element of international law, it too is subject to capricious or self-interested vetoes, worth about as much as the paper it is printed on. As a case in point, all efforts by the UN to find durable solutions to the Arab–Israel conflict are in vain if the veto prevents the resolutions from becoming binding. Consequently, the number of unresolved conflicts around the world continues to increase, piling up in the Security Council's "pending tray," waiting for solutions.

Herein lies the paradox. The international institution created in the aftermath of the Second World War to address threats to world peace and security and to promote economic and social development is all too often rendered toothless during crises. On the one hand, you have approved resolutions that are deprived of practical application, and on the other, you have conflicts where the belligerents are unaccountable. If belligerents can secure the support of at least one member of the Permanent Five willing to exercise the veto, they can act with impunity as far as the UN is concerned. A straight answer would be to reform or do away with the veto power granted to the Permanent Five. Of course, the Permanent Five themselves would need to acquiesce if the Security Council, in particular, and the United Nations, in general, are to work in an effective way to address global conflicts and crises, as the world public expects that they should.

Conclusions

Since it came into being in 1945, the UN has tried hard to defend the world from the many military, economic, environmental, and health crises it has faced. Although some of these crises have not been solved, the UN is still capable of acting with vigor when it is given the chance. Unfortunately, despite continuous efforts for the last seventy-seven years, getting that chance is not always possible. The factors that incapacitate the UN with respect to crisis response are themselves abundant. However, the most significant factor is that the hands of the UN are regularly tied by its own membership.

Although the UN has the exclusive prerogative and clear mandate, all too often, national interests flagrantly or subtly interfere with the system's ability to fulfill its legitimate functions with respect to the resolution of conflicts and other global crises. Efforts to address conflicts and other crises are scattered across a complex UN System, which is hamstrung not only by the veto power of permanent members of the Security Council but also by the fact that the influence of national governments reverberates through the entire decision-making apparatus.

Other mechanisms besides the P5 veto that hobble the UN's ability to function include "the power of the purse," which cannot be discounted as unimportant.

If one member's financial contribution to the budget of the UN is sizable, they can often dictate conditions for those contributions (which may or may not be transparent to outside observers or even some insiders). Furthermore, regional rivalries, such as the Arab–Israeli conflict and the conflict between India and Pakistan, spill over into the decision matrices of the UN. Likewise, ideological conflicts between right-wing and left-wing regimes in Latin America, themselves echoes of the Cold War era rivalries of Eastern and Western blocs, remain relevant within the corridors of multilateralism. Lastly, the influence that stronger countries hold over weaker countries is not limited to bilateral relations. They inevitably spill over into decision-making at the United Nations, where the votes of weaker countries are, if not for sale, at least for rent.

It is hardly surprising that sensible decisions often cannot be made or that sane solutions flounder in such an unhealthy environment. The situation calls for an urgent revision of the way the UN operates and for a subsequent resolution by the political organ of the UN where all members are represented, namely, the General Assembly. That is where the question of making the organization more responsive to its mandate and more effective in its crisis responses should be debated. To accomplish this, the distinction between the nonbinding resolutions of the General Assembly and the binding resolutions of the Security Council must be done away with, or the UN will continue to drag its feet in its crisis response exercises. But alas, the authority to make this change is vested in the Security Council and, ultimately, in the five permanent members, who have the power to veto any proposed changes to the UN Charter. And so, even when a permanent member is not directly responsible for blocking a crisis response, they are indirectly responsible for the organizational situation that allows better intentions to descend into a stalemate.

Notes

1 UN Security Council, Resolution 1239, on relief assistance to Kosovo refugees and internally displaced persons in Kosovo, the Republic of Montenegro, and other parts of Yugoslavia, S/RES/1239 (1999), May 14, 1999, https://digitallibrary.un.org/record/1493988?v=pdf; and UN Security Council,

Resolution 1244, on the deployment of international civil and security presences in Kosovo, S/RES/1244 (1999), June 10, 1999, https://digitallibrary.un.org/record/274488?v=pdf.

2 S/RES/1239(1999).

3 S/RES/1244(1999).

4 Report of the Secretary-General pursuant to General Assembly resolution 53/35: #the fall of Srebrenica, 108, https://digitallibrary.un.org/record/372298.

5 David Bosco, "When the Blue Helmets Are to Blame," Foreign Policy (July 22, 2014).

6 UN General Assembly, Resolution 74/270, Global solidarity to fight the coronavirus disease 2019 (COVID-19), A/RES/74/270 (April 3, 2020).

7 UN Security Council, Resolution 2532, On cessation of hostilities in the context of the coronavirus disease (COVID-19) pandemic, S/RES/2532, July 1, 2020, https://digitallibrary.un.org/record/3870751?v=pdf.

8 Simon Tisdall, "The United Nations Has the Power to Punish Putin. This Is How It Can Be Done," *The Guardian* (April 6, 2022), https://www.theguardian.com/commentisfree/2022/apr/06/united-nations-putin-ukraine-catastrophic.

9 Tisdall, "The United Nations Has the Power to Punish Putin. This Is How It Can Be Done."

10 UN Security Council, Resolution 773, Draft resolution on humanitarian pauses in Israel-Gaza conflict, S/2023/773, October 18, 2023.

5

Financing the United Nations

The main source of the funds that are necessary for administering the bureaucracy of the United Nations and for executing the work of the main organs of the organization and its programs in various fields essentially comes from the members. The mandatory dues are justified by the fact that they are full members of the System, and contributions are calculated based on the GDP of each member state. Additionally, and to a lesser extent, funds come from voluntary contributions from several sources: governments, businesses, or individuals.

Contributions finance the work of the United Nations proper in New York City as well as that of the fifteen specialized agencies, each having its own budget. The burden created by these annual fees weighs heavily on member states, especially those with medium- and low-performing economies. Consequently, it is not unusual to hear that states are in arrears. Article 19 of the charter notes that states that are in arrears for the preceding two years, or owe the equivalent of two years' worth of dues, lose their right to vote in the General Assembly. However, the final sentence of that article opens a door of hope for desperate nations by stating that "The General Assembly may, nevertheless, permit such a Member to vote if it is satisfied that the failure to pay is due to conditions beyond the control of the Member."[1] A sizable number of member states simply cannot afford to pay their dues, which can amount to millions of dollars, to the UN. Therefore, one can sometimes see delegates of pardoned states, running to the Assembly Secretariat before the session begins to present the written letter of exemption so that they can exercise their right to vote. Ultimately, the arrears do need to be paid, and so member states borrow the money. This is a self-defeating exercise that entails the unwarranted consequences of debt servicing, currency devaluation, and, in the worst scenario, placing their economies at the mercy of the lenders, including the Bretton Woods Institutions. Borrowing has a calamitous effect on the future of the states concerned.

The main budget of the United Nations proper is a straightforward expenditure relating to the organization of meetings, conferences, and seminars held at the headquarters by the organs of the United Nations and their subsidiaries. The main and specialized programs are headquartered elsewhere but operate according to decisions taken at the New York City United Nations Tower that pertain either to all member states or to specific specialized agencies. Like many multilateral organizations, the agencies have grown with time and have widened their scope of activities and recruited more staff, and as a result have either outgrown or bloated their size, staff, and budget. However, the United Nations was able to adapt itself to this situation, unfavorable though it might seem. It has trailed other organizations for many reasons not entirely of its own making, but still within its auspices. Therefore, the increase in size, staff, and budget could be considered numerical. UNESCO is a case in point.

It has been said all along in the writing of this book that there are opportunities for waste, fraud, and the mismanagement of the finances of the United Nations. However, these problems cannot possibly be avoided simply because of the size of the System and the number of member states it serves, compounded by the constant growth in the scope of activities and its financial considerations. However, such opportunities are a by-product of this growth and not the main determinant of the phenomenon. The main defect that is at the base of all financial problems the United Nations System encounters is structural. To begin with, the United Nations has no independent source of financing that would enable the organization to take independent decisions relating to its work. It forms its budget from contributions coming from its member states and on voluntary contributions—again from member states—like those going to UNICEF. It is therefore understandable that those states that pay more, whether obligatory or voluntarily, will have more influence in shaping the United Nations decision-making process in a way that will benefit them. This is particularly true when it comes to the Bretton Woods Institutions, whose hands are often tied by the source of their funding. Had the United Nations possessed its own separate financial system, it would be free to do whatever it takes to serve the needs and interests of contributing member states in a collective rather than individual manner and to provide control and accountability.

Another issue with the United Nations financing model concerns contributions that come from low- or moderate-income member states. This is where the continuous growth of the System hits hard. The problem that faces these states is twofold. First, they cannot cope with the constantly increasing amount of their obligatory contributions that results from the constant growth of the System because their limited economies do not sustain such a continuous growth. Second, they expect a reasonable return from their contributions in the form of United Nations development assistance, which is not always guaranteed. In the end, the problem of the United Nations financing is structural because member states are borrowing money to pay their dues and then relying on the United Nations to spend that money on much-needed projects in their respective countries. They could instead use the money earmarked or borrowed for UN contributions to finance compelling national projects of their own.

UNESCO, as the name indicates, started with education, science, and culture but has since added communication and development, which has resulted in increasing its headquarters buildings from three to five—and that does not even consider the seven affiliates. This growth has meant a corresponding increase in staff to take care of the acquired mandates. This overgrowth within and beyond UNESCO has created room for possible duplications and overlaps. For example, Part One of the 2020–1 Program and Budget appropriated $20 million for staff working in general policy and direction, while only $2 million was allocated to operational programming. In Part Three, which deals with corporate services, the staff budget surpassed the operational budget by $35 million. Money from other agencies and funds is also involved. For instance, UNESCO's work overlaps with the Commission for Sustainable Development and the United Nations Development Programme (UNDP) when it deals with the subject of sustainable development in its National Sciences sector. UNESCO also touches on climate change, which overlaps in part with the United Nations Environment Programme (UNEP). UNESCO also overlaps with other agencies, for instance with the Commission on Human Rights, when it takes on matters related to human rights and gender; or in the case of the Commission on the Status of Women, where the work overlaps with work done by the Board of Trustees of the International Research and Training Institute for the Advancement of Women and possibly the United Nations Development Fund.

Some might argue that each agency, commission, or fund handles matters that pertain to its own specialization; however, the subject is the same. It would be more effective and economical to centralize the administration of similar subjects in one organ. That lessens the financial burden on member states and eases the budgets of these organs. One could argue that the increase in the number of international staff opens the door for more recruitment from member states and that this compensates in an indirect way for their financial contributions to the United Nations organs, but the overlap hurts the effectiveness and quality of the programs.

Finally, overlapping is partly the result of a lack of coordination among the organs because everybody is trying to keep their independence from each other. This drive for independence leads to overlapping and a loss of money and time—just like what happens nationally in the ministries of member states.

If the overlapping of functions and focal areas within the UN System exists to ensure full coverage of its mandate, then perhaps it can be a positive feature. However, the reasons for the overlapping are not full coverage but overgrowing, duplication, overstaffing, and over-reaching. As previously mentioned, the three remedies for addressing these challenges are full decentralization, transfer of some Head Quarters functions to the field, and the amalgamation of offices and programs that are similar in nature. On the other hand, if one specialized agency took care of all responsibilities for an area within the UN mandate, this may be going to the other extreme side, i.e., full centralization. The suggested middle course is more suitable and likely more effective.

Like any mega organization, the United Nations has negative features that result from its size, but the United Nations is the most international and comprehensive of such organizations, and this makes the problems worse than in any other organization. Yet nobody seems to have the enthusiasm or the intention to do something about the ills that the UN suffers from.

To recap, the main areas of concern when it comes to financing are overgrowing, duplication, overlapping, overstaffing, over-stretching, and having too many headquarters. To effect fundamental and effective change, the UN needs to decentralize fully, transfer headquarters to the field, and amalgamate some areas of operation.

Stage 1—Decentralize Fully

At present, agencies have field offices to supervise the execution of these agencies' programs in the developing countries where assistance is needed. However, the decisions on what work to carry out are taken at headquarters in Europe, Canada, or the United States. This should change for the benefit of the programs by delegating at least some power of action to those working in the field. For example, UNESCO has field offices for education, while FAO has field offices for agriculture. There is no reason why we cannot combine the two stages necessary for any program, i.e., planning and execution, under one roof. Think of the savings in staff, money, and time that could result from combining two field offices. Additionally, the quality of the programming will be enhanced by a more efficient use of logistics, people, and working conditions. Think, for example, of any educational program operating in Kenya while the planning and decisions for execution happen in Paris. This disconnect happens not only in the case of the major five specialized agencies but also with smaller specialized entities. The European headquarters should only handle the overall policies and plans of the agency in question. People in the field know better the nature of the problems involved, and hence they are in a better position to judge the sustainability of program plans for the local conditions and therefore the right course of action to follow and execute.

Stage 2—The Gradual Transfer of Headquarters to the Field

This means combining the headquarters and the field offices into a single unit, centered in the field, that is, the location where the United Nations provides developmental assistance to countries in Asia, Africa, Latin America, and the Oceanic Islands. The current situation, concentrating agency headquarters in Europe, is not optimal and is yet another example of the United Nations' failure to adapt. Locating the headquarters in Europe made sense in the aftermath of the Second World War when Europe was the field for reconstruction and development. Since then, the focus of developmental assistance has shifted to developing countries outside Europe, and the rationale for locating headquarters in Europe no longer holds. Headquarters should be located in the same region as the field offices, as they were after the Second World War. Locating the headquarters and the field offices in one place all in the field has two clear advantages: the quality of the program will improve and the costs of material and staff will be more reasonable and hence bearable.

One can rightfully ask whether HQ functions would be duplicated in different field offices if agencies and programs serve multiple regions; however, this is not necessarily the case. Where there are similar programs, the headquarters can liaise among themselves, while different programs will have their own HQ. The essential point here is that planning as well as execution of programs will be done in the same place, and that efficiency outweighs the bit of overlap that might occur. After all, since all the UN specialized agencies fall under the auspices of ECOSOC, there won't be any problem concerning the general policy for the development sectors and programs.

Stage 3—Amalgamate

The UN can attain further efficiency by merging the commissions, committees, funds, and programs with the specialized agencies that do the same or nearly similar work, or have the same mandates as the agencies, and redistribute the agency HQs among the countries of Asia, Africa, and Latin America since that is where the field lies at present and for the foreseeable future. Two distinct advantages will come out of this amalgamation and redistribution: the quality of the work done will improve since it is informed at close range by the needs of the recipient nation, and there will be a clear economization of resources, material, and finances. Good quality work enhances the reputation of the United Nations, and the advantage of economizing on resources and staff is clearly an advantage. The resultant savings must be approved by the member states, and money freed up in this way will help finance the budget of the United Nations and its subsidiaries, including the specialized agencies. This is very important when it comes to member states' contributions. Unless a lasting solution can be found along the lines of the three stages mentioned in this paragraph and the preceding ones, the needy nations will continue to be stretched financially and find themselves in an almost permanent state of arrears. This pushes them to borrow money from uncompromising lending institutions that in turn threaten to hijack their economies by imposing bitterly unpopular conditions on them.

Unless the United Nations finds a way to make it easier for member states to pay their dues to the organization's several budgets, the current situation will deteriorate to the extent that some states just cannot pay their dues anymore. The solution to this acute problem cannot stop, as it so often does, at well-organized meetings filled with justifications and counter-justifications and expert analyses that result in flowery recommendations that can be classified neatly and eventually forgotten. Hopefully, we can find a practical financial mechanism that does not lack humanitarian understanding, by which member states can feel less of a burden when paying their dues to the organization. After all, it is in the interest of both member states and the United Nations that the financial contributions are paid to the latter, in full and on time.

In this chapter, we have placed great emphasis on alleviating the financial burden on member states when it comes to paying contributions to the various budgets of the System. In this regard one can perhaps point to a dream the present secretary-general of the United Nations, António Guterres, outlined when he suggested using the organization's seventy-fifth birthday in 2020 as an occasion to widen its governance to include businesses, trade unions, NGOs, cities, and regional administrations in addition to governments. It was an attempt to revive the United Nations so that it can adapt to a changing world. If attained, this objective can break the monopoly national governments have over multinational institutions, an abnormal situation that the secretary-general and many others, including me, have observed. He is not wrong when he notes that this archaic phenomenon constitutes one of the major obstacles to the organization's efforts to reform and adapt.

If business can be involved in the governance of the United Nations, it opens a vast reservoir of financial sources from the private sector, thus lessening the burden on member states. Businesses donate large amounts to charity, and while it might seem strange to think that the United Nations, with all its sophisticated financial systems, including those of the Bretton Woods Institutions, can benefit from charity, it is not a huge stretch of the imagination. When it comes to development assistance, the noble objectives of the United Nations are tempting for charity donations because ultimately the organization is working to better the lives of citizens in its member states—and bettering lives is a key principle behind charity donations. The United Nations should not feel embarrassed to embark on this road because receiving voluntary contributions is not a strange concept within the System. In fact, some of its subsidiaries depend partially or totally on this—a case in point being UNICEF, which depends totally on voluntary contributions. Receiving charity money and using it in an organized way and under proper control for developing projects beneficial to member states has vivid advantages. Accepting charitable donations would go a long way toward making the secretary-general's dream, and ours, come true.

Concluding Thoughts

Under the auspices of the mother organization, which is the United Nations headquarters based in New York City, there are nearly fifty specialized organizations, commissions, committees, programs, and funds. Their headquarters are scattered around the world, although the bulk of them are in Europe, and their budgets amount to billions of dollars annually. These organizations recruit thousands of employees, and it takes an extensive system of control and oversight to manage where, when, and how budgeted funds are allocated and spent. Given the sheer size of the system, and human nature, there is bound to be some overlap, redundancy, and mission creep. However, it is worth remembering that the UN System was not created to benefit the organization financially but for the purpose of executing the UN development programs in its member states. Considering the huge amounts of money available, the risks of overspending and underperforming, or even outright graft and corruption, cannot be ruled out. It is therefore worth noting again how important it is to have an effective system of control sustained by a rigorous follow-up procedure after program execution is complete. Currently, oversight units are scattered around various sections and departments and around the world. The remedy is to have a *centralized audit, assessment, and accountability unit* that monitors an otherwise decentralized and widely distributed system. This unit should be permanent and placed high up in the hierarchy of the Secretariat, with satellite offices embedded in various UN organs and organizations. Above all, it should have a high degree of operational autonomy and a direct channel of communication with the secretary-general. Only then will coherence and efficiency prevail in program development and execution and UN work in general.

The suggestion of having a centralized audit, assessment, and accountability unit is not a luxury for an organization as large and decentralized as the United Nations. Without such a unit, member states will inevitably lose confidence in the ability of the UN to fulfill its development mission, and the funds that currently support UN programs will not be diverted to finance national development projects or international projects initiated out of national self-interest.

Note

1 The full text of the UN Charter is available at https://www.un.org/en/about-us/un-charter/full-text.

6

Reforming the United Nations System

Reforming any system is a multifaceted operation, and the bigger the outfit, the more varied and complicated the approach becomes. There are certain fundamental elements for a reform process to be productive. It should be preceded by and based on a sound, continuous follow-up of what is being done with a parallel exercise in evaluation. In the absence of such a solid base, reform will be shaky and unproductive. But reform is more comprehensive than follow-up and evaluation. Reform takes care of the whole system, while follow-up and evaluation handle a set of projects. The two processes are interrelated: qualitative reform cannot be secured without a sound follow-up and effective evaluation.

Applied to reforming the United Nations System, this means knowing precisely what the hurdles are that stand in the way of or prevent the reform process because you have to know the problem before you think of the proper solution.

First, we need to know whether those who will and can effect reform really mean to do so or whether they are using the noble idea as a figure of speech to hide another agenda. We need to know if they are playing for time or wasting it to serve that hidden purpose, especially if the reform will result in depriving them of any advantages they possess at present. In essence, will they politicize reform at the United Nations by subjecting it to complications and dead ends that will ultimately render the process of reforming useless? Therefore, we need to explore the underlying reasons for appearing to want reform while in fact trying to block it. Take the matter of decentralizing operations so that programs are controlled in the field where the problems are being treated. The European capitals that house headquarters away from the field might resist the transfer for obvious economic and social reasons, even though they know that they can no longer justify hosting those headquarters from an operational standpoint. Their argument that the developing countries that seek assistance and constitute the field are not fit to host the headquarters does not hold ground because those countries have attained a reasonable standard of development since 1945 and are suitable hosts.

The second hurdle is finding a way to overcome national interests in favor of a multinational approach when it comes to UN affairs. This thinking and approach will be based on marked contradiction between nationalism and multilateralism when one method is used to solve a problem by the other. When a particular government proposes a development plan within its country's boundaries, the yardstick is not the same as it would be for the United Nations Organization or its subsidiaries in the field—not in terms of size, resources, or conditions on the ground—and applying those standards to an international scenario will not work. No fruitful reform of the UN can result if representatives give priority to national interests. When it comes to reforming the UN, the problem is that the international staff who will be engaged in the reform process depend on the resources of national governments. What's more, the representatives who will make decisions on United Nations reforms come from those governments that harbor nationalist tendencies. An international organization does not function in the same way that countries run their national institutions. Ideally, the solution lies in having separate outfits in the capital working only for United Nations affairs. While this situation does in fact exist in some affluent countries that can afford it, there is not enough freedom of action: decision-making still must go to national affairs in the government hierarchy. National commissions or departments for United Nations affairs that exist in member states are mainly advisory and powerless. Since the money for the United Nations budget comes from member states, there is no way to resolve this contradiction unless the United Nations develops its own monetary scheme.

The third hurdle is related to the size of the System. There are 193 member nations and many programs and agencies that fall under the UN. The regular budget alone amounts to three billion US dollars, not to mention that peacekeeping and the specialized agencies each have their own budget and staff. The colossal amount of money that is circulated, the numerous building headquarters, the number and variety of programs executed, and the number of staff doing the job make reforming the System almost impossible. Paradoxically, it is precisely because of the size of the organization and its derivatives that reform needs to happen. As a result, the size of the System has become the pretext for constantly delaying the process or running away from it altogether. From the outside, it might seem as if changes have been made, but this is not the same thing as reform—and reform has not happened. A process as big and comprehensive as overhauling the System needs to be done in stages.

A fourth hurdle is that although the System's economic and social programs are international in character and design, they are subjected to approval by national governments, which again presents a paradox when nationalism is supposed to be in service of multilateralism when it comes to UN affairs. What aggravates this situation is that for three-quarters of a century, the System has been almost stagnant, crippled by what the victors put in the charter to prevent another major war. Article 108 of the charter is clear: any envisaged reform will entail an amendment of the charter, and that will not be possible without the approval of two-thirds of members of the General Assembly, including all the permanent members of the Security Council. And as we know only too well, the Permanent Five have the right to veto any proposal. The result is virtual paralysis of the System while the world changes. It is not an easy task to amend the charter of the United Nations, including Article 108, so that the road to reform is cleared. There have been a few attempts to amend the charter, but these efforts stopped for some reason. We do not know, for example, whether the veto holders used their veto power to back their wishes to negotiate further amendments to reform the United Nations. We know that the General Assembly has constituted reform panels in the past, but no continuous negotiations have been undertaken with the Permanent Five to know what they are thinking. We know the routine of commissions and committees' work and deliberations, but this falls short of fruitful negotiations with the parties concerned. There are no current attempts to discuss reform, and we are treating the Permanent Five as untouchable, even though they are humans like us and represent governments like ours despite their leverage.

Given all these hurdles that hamper the operations of the United Nations, will reforms be possible? The answer is yes with a capital *Y*. Because of these hurdles, reforming the System is no longer an option but an urgent necessity. It is just that the difficulties seem insurmountable, and the number of reform-related issues that need attention is innumerable. Reforms should not be restricted to the Security Council but should include the whole System's main and subsidiary organs. In fact, it might be recommended that reforming the United Nations Security Council should be delayed until after the rest of the System has been reformed. All the organs of the System have been dormant for a long time, and the whole exercise of reform will be long and tedious, even if it is necessary and urgent.

Where and what to reform is the seven-billion-dollar question, and the figure here is hardly exaggerated because the sum of the budgets of the main organization and its subsidiaries runs into billions of dollars annually or biannually. The United Nations System is the biggest outfit in the world, just as it was when it was put into operation three-quarters of a century ago; it was bound to further outgrow itself. Reviews to correct oversight have proved to be insufficient, and even making follow-up part of any program execution will not be enough. There should be an independent body (or bodies) whose sole responsibility is to review and evaluate the System's program application. The independent review outfit must be part of the organization but separate from its organs because being part of the System means it would know the System's operations much better than any other outside ad hoc committee, seminar, or retreat that the secretary-general undertakes, like now and then inviting outside officials or experts to look at the United Nations' performance. Furthermore, independent internal reviews and evaluations should not stop at final reports but should suggest practical steps to improve performance.

The independent outfit should be multidisciplinary, and we hesitate to use the adjective here because it is familiar jargon in the dictionaries of multipurpose commissions and committees. These bodies spend their meeting time going through lengthy discussions only to come up with nothing substantial, let alone tangible and far-reaching in its mandate. An independent review body needs to work differently—there needs to be less discussion and more practical, applicable recommendations.

One might ask why we should have this inside-outside outfit. Because without it, how are we going to control such a diverse and multidisciplinary organization like the United Nations, which is rich in resources but with scattered activities all over the globe and housed in a huge number of buildings manned by thousands of individuals? Control is not the end of the story; there must be a way to evaluate the work of this independent review body. However, if we are going to give this outfit a limited mandate, resources, time limits, and above all, restrict its power, it will become just another commission or committee mounted by the organization in the course of its work. Put simply, the outfit should be alive and listened to. Without it, the work of the organization risks falling into a state of not knowing what is done, when, where, and why. Perhaps that explains the shaky position and state of the United Nations at present.

Where and what to reform first will depend on the approach, but what is clear is that reform should encompass the entire System with all its organs, agencies, funds, and programs. The temptation is to start with the Security Council and to do something about the veto power and permanent membership of the council, but such an approach will almost certainly terminate early as a result of that veto. The sensible thing to do is to begin with the other organs outside the Security Council and to leave the latter to the end. This approach will make possible reforms that will not breach the text of the charter and allow for a series of positive results on which further reforms can be built. Eventually, one will reach the inevitable, i.e., reform of the Security Council.

Before embarking on a discussion of specific reforms, we need to address the dilemma of whether representatives of the UN are working for the international system or prioritizing their national interests. The United Nations family is represented by the organization, which is multilateral, while states are represented by their governments that prioritize national interests. Member states are part of the United Nations, an organization that transcends national boundaries, and therefore they are complementary to the system as a whole. However, what we see at present is the opposite. Member states prioritize their own individual interests rather than those of the United Nations as a whole. Hence, we witness rivalries and contradictions that affect the workings of the United Nations adversely. That makes the international system incapable of asserting and maintaining peace and security in the world. If a complementary relationship between the United Nations and its member states is the norm, a positive atmosphere will permit both sides to function better. More needs to be done within member states to inculcate a culture of complementary relations with the United Nations in the general public. Member states need to embark on information drives and address the role and position of the United Nations on every level, including the classroom. Only a change in mentality can secure suitable terrain for a productive reform.

Such an information drive can only be successful if the United Nations does its part by becoming more open and transparent about its workings. Information about United Nations operations should be circulated freely and willingly with as little secrecy as possible. However, this does not seem to be the case as there have been incidents that reveal the existence of a cloud of secrecy around the Secretariat. A past secretary-general, Kofi Annan, admitted as much that the United Nations must open up and that the Secretariat should not be hiding any information from other United Nations organs such as the General Assembly, the Security Council, ECOSOC, and the like. There should not be secrecy regarding information about departments within the United Nations, and at the same time we should expect better dissemination of information about the United Nations to external stakeholders.

It seems that the Department of Information at the United Nations Tower in New York City is doing more than a satisfactory job of making information available through its numerous bureaus around the world. However, stop anybody in a government house, parliament building, or the street for that matter, and ask about the United Nations, and the reply will be "I don't know." Compare this with the constant flow of information about what is happening nationally in the country. If countries advocate the multilateralism of the United Nations more prominently, for instance, by setting aside time in their media to air information about the United Nations and its subsidiaries, this might change. However, as things stand, information about the UN is not reaching the street.

One major comprehensive reform that needs to be addressed is finding a suitable balance between a program and the cost of executing that plan. Otherwise, program costs will make initiatives too expensive to sustain. The emphasis is placed here on staff cost because they are the people who will create and manage the programs in the United Nations member states. This balance between programming and cost is important for any institution because it is proof of its sound management. If the funds allocated for the salaries exceed those set aside for programs, there is a problem of management, and the institution becomes a recruiting powerhouse. Of course, staff salaries sustain families, but programs have the priority and not the other way round. Vigilance and scrutiny are essential as institutions and responsibilities grow, and an outfit as large as the United Nations and its subsidiaries, funds, and programs needs more oversight than most. Of late, the United Nations organizations have taken steps to try to keep the balance between staff remuneration and program costs, but given the sheer size of the organization and the number of staff involved, such scrutiny should be undertaken on a more regular basis and by independent bodies within the System. This becomes more important when the scrutiny is related to the responsibility of the United Nations member states to honor their commitment of paying their contributions to the budget of the organization and its subsidiaries. For rich countries, paying their dues poses no problem, but for countries with smaller economies, it is difficult to do so, if not impossible. Some of the poorer countries send partial payments so that they do not lose their voting rights at the General Assembly, but it often means they end up with a permanent debt to the organization.

As to the reform of the Security Council, it is important and at the same time problematic because the structure of the council presents a major hurdle. The existence of the Permanent Five with veto powers was meant to prevent a third major world war, but what was intended as a blessing turned out to be a curse as it stops any attempt to make the United Nations System function better because if one of the five does not agree with a proposal, they will veto it. Regardless of how democratic the decision-making process is in other parts of the system, or how it reflects the will of the rest of the world, final approval rests in the hands of those five nations with veto power. What we have ended up with is a situation where permanent membership of the Security Council prevents a full rotation of its members and a veto power that can negate any proposal for reform. The existence of permanent membership to the council and the veto have become symbols of autocracy and dictatorship. It is hard to comprehend how, at a time when member states are always preaching about democratic rule, they can tolerate the practice of authoritarian decision-making at the United Nations Security Council.

We now turn to the three key areas in which changes need to be made to the Security Council: membership, the veto, and the way the council functions.

Changing Membership

Membership of the Security Council should change to reflect a fair proportional representation of the membership of the organization as a whole. When the United Nations was founded, there were fifty-one member states and eleven members of the Security Council; that is to say, the council comprised nearly 22 percent of the total membership (21.56 percent, to be exact). The number of council members was later increased to fifteen, the number we have today, while membership has grown to 193 nations. This means that the Security Council now represents just under 8 percent (7.77 percent) of the membership—a third of the original figure. These basic numbers are not the only metric for determining the desired proportionality, but they do give one a sense of how the balance has shifted. Changing the size and composition of the Security Council means that more member states of the United Nations will have the opportunity to participate in the deliberations and decision-making of the council. The criteria for the increase should not be based on permanent and non-permanent membership of the council, as is the case at present. We need to do away with permanent membership. Halfway solutions, such as calling for an increase in the number of non-permanent members but keeping the present Permanent Five, will not work because permanent membership remains coupled with the veto. Nor should the selection of candidates or the increase in council membership be based on the size, either of the economy or the population of member states. The allocation of seats to the five geographical groups should be also adapted to allow for the increase in membership from these regions and should include the rotation of candidatures while maintaining the present term of two years.

Changing the Veto Power

The reasons for establishing the veto and assigning it to the victors after the Second World War were noble in that they wanted to prevent another major world war. That objective has been achieved because there has not been a third war. However, regional wars are abundant—maybe not in the regions covered by these major powers but certainly in the rest of the world. What was once a blessing has turned into a curse because it has negatively affected the work of the Security Council, and it is time to abolish it. Because of the veto, the national interests of those who have that power have overshadowed the neutral role of the United Nations System and have made the council work in the service of individual interests rather than of global multilateral objectives. Furthermore, having the right of the veto and casting it is a completely discriminatory, undemocratic, and authoritarian phenomenon that runs against the principles of the United Nations Charter. Any attempt to reform the council while retaining the right of veto is meaningless: ultimate control remains with those five members. Partial reform attempts only reaffirm the power of the haves over the have-nots among the United Nations membership. There is no other way except to increase the size of the council, and in turn to increase the number of seats allocated to the five geographical groups in the United Nations. The present system for the rotation of candidatures and for membership of the council should remain. This will avoid discrimination among member states under any pretext.

Changing the Way the Council Works

Many individuals, societies, and foundations—not to mention conferences and panels—have engaged in writing to the organization or speak out and advocate for reform of the United Nations. The common cause for their exercise has been, and continues to be, the unfavorable state the organization finds itself in. Their reasoning invariably boils down to this: The way the council works should be reviewed and eventually changed because at present it allows council members to stress their national interests when they should be advocating for an internationalist approach in dealing with council matters. At present the council meets in a small, stuffy consultation room with a V-shaped table where the president sits at the head. The secretary-general or his representative sits on his right and the secretary of the council on his left, with the remaining council members distributed alphabetically on both the left-hand and the right-hand sides. The council engages in a full debate of the agenda items and at the end of the deliberations there are three kinds of conclusive actions open to the council regarding any item on its agenda: (1) a press release read by its president to the press representatives who are waiting outside; (2) a presidential statement read by the president in an open session; or (3) agreement on a draft resolution to be put to voting in an open meeting. Both the press and the presidential statements should be adopted unanimously. Draft resolutions need to obtain nine votes out of fifteen to pass, including the agreement of the Permanent Five and any objection of one or more of the latter will bury it.[1]

At present, all the work done by the council, including decision-making, happens in camera and the council does not go public except to formalize its agreement on the subject or to cast a vote on it. It is worth pointing out that in the past some of the work of the Security Council occurred in public sessions in the Council Hall that is adorned significantly by a huge tableau depicting the liberation from slavery. The public meetings were held in the presence of other members of the United Nations who are not members of the council, as well as the press core. I would recommend a return to having public meetings as part of the process of reforming the council. If meetings are held in public rather than behind closed doors, the international character of the United Nations' work is boosted, and at the same time the national tendencies—especially those stemming from the rivalry among the Permanent Five—will be suppressed. The council has recently held public meetings, but the content of these sessions is limited to general subjects like controlling small arms, child soldiers, and AIDS. No decisions are taken at these public meetings. Members and non-members are simply airing their country's opinion on these subjects.

The General Assembly, feeling the need for reforming the work and membership of the Security Council, has established a committee for this purpose. Immediately, there was a flow of contradictory claims and suggestions essentially calling for an increase in non-permanent seats, side by side with demands for an increase in the number of permanent seats. Obviously, these two proposals cancel each other. The Permanent Five gave the proposals a cool reception—for obvious reasons, because who would want to forego the two rights that they have acquired and imposed on the work of the council and other United Nations organs since the creation of the organization. As a result, the Committee on Reforms has hit a stone wall despite multiple renewals of its mandate. There is no doubt that various departments and sections of the organization have tried to amend the way they work, but amelioration cannot take the place of reforms because wherever you look in the System to reform it, you will always end up wanting the approval of the Permanent Five inside the council and outside it—Article 108 of the Charter is very clear on this.

While it seems easy to blame a lack of reform on the size of the organization, the main cause lies deeper: governance of an international organization like the United Nations is undertaken by methods identical to national governance. This has resulted in a complicated, unhealthy working atmosphere.

Among those who have attempted to remedy the situation is the conservative American Enterprise Institute for Public Policy Research. In this regard, they produced a 2005 book, authored by Joshua Muravchik, entitled *The Future of the United Nations: Understanding the Past to Chart a Way Forward.*[2] Muravchik's criticisms of the UN fall squarely in line with conservative biases against multilateralism beyond alliances of convenience and self-interest, and he spares scant and faint praise for its successes. He also finds fault, predictably, both in the UN's aspiration to be the cops of the world and its failure to fulfill this aspiration.

Muravchik takes the position that establishing the UN in the first place was a mistake. Nonetheless, given that the institution exists and is unlikely to be dismantled, Muravchik turns his attention to three familiar categories of UN reform: improving the United Nations' efficiency, enhancing its capabilities, and revising its fundamental political structures. Efficiency, Muravchik posits, can be improved by challenging the problem of overstaffing or what is called "deadwood" through buying it out, only to say that this solution is self-defeating because it will create new deadwoods, although it is recognized that they stand as hurdles to efficient United Nations operations.

By contrast, I would propose that there is another way out—abolish the aura of secrecy at the Secretariat. If discussions are open to the public, then representatives will not be inclined to push national agendas as much or to withhold information. There are many examples that show that information was withheld from the General Assembly. When the Oil-for-Food scandal broke, it was revealed that member states were not aware of fifty-five internal audits. At the time, Secretary-General Kofi Annan promised to identify categories of information and to make them available routinely. However, this sounds like a piecemeal solution that risks irregularity and will be less comprehensive than required. Moreover, identifying these categories would depend solely on one person, the secretary-general of the United Nations. The best thing to do is to adopt, via the General Assembly, something akin to a freedom of information setup that will regularize information-sharing and make access to information about the UN's business more comprehensive.

Concluding Remarks on Reforming the United Nations

Enhancing the capabilities of the United Nations has centered on peacekeeping, much of it stemming from the panel that was formed and chaired by Ambassador Lakhdar Brahimi. However, most of the recommendations made by Ambassador Brahimi have not been implemented. One good thing that has arisen from the work of that panel is that it contributed to the creation of the Peacebuilding Commission, which mainly looked at signs and potential conflicts to deal with crises before they turn into wars; in other words, preventive peacekeeping.

In its report, the panel notes that the current relation between democracy and global governance is inadequate. While the substance of politics (trade, economies, environment, pandemics, and terrorism) is globalizing, the process of politics is not because the principal institutions (elections, political parties, and parliaments) remain the affairs of national and local governments. One solution that has been suggested is to engage civil societies in global governance. This solution, which does away with government mediation, has potential, but it will be more practical if governments influence is complementary to, and not replaced by, civil societies. This is exactly what the present Secretary-General António Guterres is aspiring to do.

Revision of the political structure is justified by the fading relevance and influence of the United Nations: The General Assembly as well as the Human Rights Commission can attest to Secretary-General Annan's observation of declining public confidence in the United Nations. That decline surely includes its institutions, except perhaps the Bretton Woods Institutions, the World Bank, and the IMF. But even among these institutions, reform is necessary because the present structure favors the donors, not the receivers, when it should be the other way round.

Vesselin Popovski has proposed two alternatives for enlarging and restructuring the Security Council to make it more representative: both proposals increase the members from 15 to 24. One proposal includes six new permanent members, while the other proposes eight new seats with a renewable four-year term. Neither alternative will give a veto right to the newcomers. The changes are justified by a change in power politics in the world with the emergence of Germany, Japan, and India (Brazil is not mentioned). As Secretary-General Annan has said, the Security Council must be broadly representative of the realities of power in today's world. Given the fact that the report was commissioned by an American institution, it does not side completely with the panel's suggestions and sees them as an attempt to equate the beneficiaries with the power of the United States. It does not see the advantage of opening the Security Council and making it more democratic, and instead works to maintain the closed council where national interests of the influential members are served by and through an international organ.

Another reform attempt was made by the Council on Foreign Relations and Freedom House (American) that calls for the formation of a "Democracy Caucus" at the United Nations. It entails the cooperation of all democracies around the world for the purpose of running the United Nations. However, fear of the United States' dominance as a leader of democracies has put some limits on the suggestion, though it could contribute to strengthening the peacekeeping work of the United Nations in highlighting some success in conflict prevention with a marked reduction in civil wars.

Evoking the question of state sovereignty vis-à-vis international intervention through the Security Council in the event of an armed attack on that state, the Panel notes that

> History teaches us all too clearly that it cannot be assumed that every state will always be able, or willing, to meet its responsibilities to protect its own people. And in those circumstances, the principles of those responsibilities should be taken up by the international community.[3]

This quotation refers to Article 51 of the United Nations Charter, which authorizes any member state that has been a victim of an attack to take individual or collective action to repel that attack with the imperative knowledge and subsequent intervention of the Security Council. Adding the full support of the panel and Secretary-General Annan, we note that this applied to the liberation of Kuwait in 1991 but not to the American attack on Saddam Hussein's Iraq in 2003 because the latter attack was not sanctioned by the Security Council. The United Nations undertakes "preventive" measures for peace and security, while the American interpretation centers around taking "pre-emptive" actions.

Having referred to a report on reforming the System of the United Nations from a skeptical outsider to the organization, i.e., the American Enterprise Institute, we turn to another one by way of comparison and complementarity, this time from the South Centre which has put itself in the service of the developing countries even though it is based in Geneva (Switzerland) so that we have two voices, one from a developed influential country and another from the assistance-receiving side.

The report is titled *Meeting the Challenges of UN Reform: A South Perspective*, issued in August 2006. Although it is fifteen years old, no major reform(s) have taken place that make its content redundant. The report deals with the background, issues, and areas of United Nations reforms and ends with recommendations addressed to the developing countries. However, there are a number of important points (issues) worth dwelling on. In part two of the report, major issues are mentioned that constitute a challenge to reforms, namely, sovereignty of states, the North–South divide, and growing inequality. These challenges are mentioned in the context of reforms that will enhance global governance with the United Nations at the helm because it is the legitimate and sole representative organization entrusted with running world affairs relating to peacekeeping, economic, and social development. It is obvious here that the developing countries want to have a role in the process of reforming the United Nations, drawing attention to their progress in political and social development in a changing world. The irritation of the developing countries is made clear in the heading title of one of their recommendations: "Preventing Abuse of the Power of the Purse." It is an obvious reference to the major financial contributors to the United Nations budget who have abducted the organization and held it hostage to serve their national interests. The following which comes to justify the developing countries' stand on this issue:

> Any abuse of the power of developed countries over the purse strings of the UN should be immediately met with vigorous action to remind members that the UN is a multilateral organization with developed and developing countries and that a member state's authority and responsibility to participate in the decision-making process of the UN are not limited by the amount that it contributes. Under the UN Charter, all member states are equal within bodies of the United Nations.[4]

They go as far as saying that the United Nations should not accept voluntary or donor contributions to avoid influence or conditionality. In this book, we have suggested a United Nations financial scheme that will guarantee its independence in decision-making. All this literature regarding reform signals a big difference in opinion and stance between developed and developing countries on reforming the United Nations, and unless this gap is addressed, a true and productive process of reform cannot be undertaken. In the end, the receivers (developing countries seeking assistance from the United Nations) are stressing the global governance aspect of the United Nations, while the donors (major contributors, developed countries) are resisting that push for power-sharing with the United Nations. It is a fundamental divide between the two sides that will not be easy to resolve and therefore becomes a stumbling block to reforms.

On a positive, constructive note and with a good intention of reforming the United Nations System for the benefit of both sides, the two should meet, discuss, and come up with a common approach, modest as it might be. For a start, that will develop into a full-fledged plan of action. In other words, this is to say that the two sides should put all their differences on other United Nations issues aside and constitute a separate dialogue on reforms and do away with the pretext that the issues themselves are interwoven. The countries of the South are saying that they have grown up, developed, and changed for the better. Therefore, they want their due role in the process of reforming the organization. They base their demand on the support of Secretary-General Kofi Annan's active involvement in reforming the United Nations to adapt, as he says, to a world with changing power and emphasis.

In comparing the two reports, one notes that the American report does not contain recommendations that have not been tackled before, nor does it advance practical tangible suggestions, except maybe for the Democratic Caucus. It is rather conservative in its tone and thinking that all major reforms presented by others should try to align them with American influence in the United Nations activities. This belief is based originally on the pretext that the United Nations will affect adversely America's independence in its decision-making. The report of the South Centre, by comparison, is evoking the progress that the developing countries have attained since the creation of the United Nations in 1945, and that progress puts them in a position where they want to participate actively in the process of reforming the organization. The South Centre report touches upon the same elements as the American report, i.e., strengthening the General Assembly, increasing the type and numbers of membership in the Security Council, and dealing with the peacekeeping and peacebuilding roles of the United Nations. However, the approach of the two reports to reforms is different, one essentially coming from a donor country (the highest contributor to the United Nations budget) and the other from the assistance-receiving countries, who seek "a say" in the organization's reform process based on a belief that they are not currently being heard and consulted enough, and that their participation is not sought.

A third interesting reference that can be made, this time exclusively on reforming the Security Council, is the 2015 background paper, *Reforming and Innovating the United Nations Security Council*, prepared by Vesselin Popovski for the Commission on Global Security Justice and

Governance at The Hague Institute for Global Justice. The paper's concrete recommendations are:

1. A General Assembly resolution allowing immediate re-election of retiring Security Council members by reviewing the last line of Article 23 (paragraph 2) of the charter.
2. A General Assembly resolution expanding the membership to twenty-four members.
3. A Security Council Presidential Statement containing a Code of Conduct: The Permanent Five refrain from casting the veto in situations where innocent lives are at deadly risks.
4. A General Assembly resolution reviving the "Uniting for Peace" interpretations of the General Assembly's powers that became customary international law. By adopting A/RES/377A approved by a two-thirds majority, the General Assembly gave itself the power of taking the actions necessary to restore international peace and security when the Security Council fails to take such action. By this resolution the General Assembly assumes ultimate, rather than secondary, responsibility for matters of peace and security.
5. Periodic Consultation with Civil Society and Business. The Security Council has refrained from consultation with them in its work of maintaining international peace and security, which is necessary, especially in non-traditional security threats like AIDS, Ebola, climate change, and COVID-19.[5]

Of equal importance to the paper's specific recommendations are its broader conclusions about the place of Security Council reform within the context of the overall reform of the United Nations. Acknowledging that some view Security Council reform "as the 'Holy Grail' of UN reform, whereas others treat it as an unattainable goal that diverts intellectual energy and political capital away from more pressing global governance objectives," the paper makes a compelling, pragmatic case for combining Security Council reform with other reform strategies, arguing that in this way "the unimaginable becomes possible and a potential Security Council reform can actually serve to reinforce, rather than hinder, a broader agenda for change."[6] As the concluding chapter explains, we generally side with and support this conclusion.

An enlarged Security Council would certainly be more representative of the world of twenty-first century; it will reflect the modern realities and allow states with large peacemaking, peacekeeping, and peacebuilding capacities a closer role in the decision-making, maintaining peace and security. The legitimacy gap will be filled not simply by enlarging the membership, but also by reforming the working methods toward accountability, consistency, and transparency and allowing more inclusive participation of the global civil society and business sector. A reform of the Security Council will be both a result and a signal for deeper multilateralism and can trigger reforms in other parts of the United Nations System that also need transformative changes.

It should be noted here that all the ingredients for reforming the United Nations have been referred to in the various meetings and conferences that were organized for this purpose with the participation of all concerned, inside and outside the United Nations. Yet no productive strategies and outcomes have shown themselves, first and foremost due to a lack of genuine constructive intentions on the part of the mainly big influential member states.

Notes

1 See Article 27, paragraph 3 of the Charter, https://www.un.org/en/about-us/un-charter/full-text.

2 Joshua Muravchik, *The Future of The United Nations: Understanding the Past to Chart a Way Forward*. Washington, DC: AEI Press, 2008.

3 United Nations Peacebuilding Commission, *A More Secure World: Our Shared Responsibility. Report of the High-level Panel on Threats, Challenges and Change*. New York: UN, 2004, 17.

4 The South Centre Analytical Note, *Meeting the Challenges of UN Reform: A South Perspective*. Geneva: The South Centre, August 2006, 28, https://www.southcentre.int/wp-content/uploads/2013/07/AN_GPG1_UN-Reform-South-Perspective_EN.pdf.

5 Vesselin Popovski, "Reforming and Innovating the United Nations Security Council," Background paper prepared for the Commission on Global Security Justice & Governance, The Hague Institute for Global Justice, 2015, 10–11, https://www.stimson.org/wp-content/files/Commission_BP_Popovski1.pdf.

6 Popovsky, "Reforming and Innovating the United Nations Security Council," 12.

7

Concluding Recommendations

The United Nations train has been running for a long time, long enough to know that some of the tracks it runs on are as old as the train itself and, like the train, need repair. The general public's interest in the train and its trips is receding, and therefore, it is time to repair and modernize both the train and its tracks before people lose interest completely. Given how long this unfavorable situation has existed, updating the system will not be easy, well-nigh impossible, though it is a must if the organization wants to stand a chance of restoring passengers' faith and interest in a practical and effective way.

The extent to which citizens in UN member states accept and recognize the United Nations depends on the degree of knowledge they have of the organization's work and the importance of that work to their daily life. At present, their knowledge of the organization does not match the level needed for a satisfactory return on their states' financial contributions. We asked a retired strategist banker about the United Nations—a middle-of-the-road choice: someone who is not too busy attending to daily life to be overly interested in the United Nations and not someone who might be knowledgeable, like a political scientist.

Our strategist banker had occupied the post of vice-chairman in a national bank in a member state. The choice had several advantages: The man was dealing with planning rather than money-counting; he knew how the government system works, he had an idea about the mentality of businessmen who seek to borrow for investment, and finally, he had an idea about the bank's general clientele and their attitude. Having retired, the investment banker read books either out of interest or to avoid the stress of self-isolation caused by COVID-19. When we asked him what he thought of the United Nations, his answer was straightforward: it is an organization that is not independent, and he stressed the importance of independence in doing its work. It is an organization, he continued, that is highly politicized in everything it does, and its decisions are influenced and dictated by big countries, especially those who have the veto. As a result, America stops decisions that are against Israel, and Russia stands against America. The two big countries—and now China has joined them—govern the United Nations. The organization's institutions, he added, did not achieve their development goals and thus did not eradicate poverty.

In other words, the United Nations has become a symbol, not a reality. Take COVID-19, for instance: The United Nations did not face this crisis in a meaningful way. The dominance of the big countries over the organization is no excuse for the shortcomings of its management, which failed to develop an effective role for the organization. Our banker's responses about the United Nations reveal that he knows and follows the news about the United Nations keenly enough to judge it, and his judgment is not favorable. But it is not hopeless, because he spells out the three basic elements that are required for reforming the organization, namely that the plan for reformation should include (a) where we are now, (b) what our targets are, and (c) how we will go about realizing them.

How can one reform a System that has failed to adapt for three-quarters of a century and is plagued by bureaucracy, overlapping of agencies, rigid budgets, and inflated size? And when, furthermore, its member states treat the work this organization does as an extension of their national interests rather than deal with it in a multinational way that concerns the whole world. Finally, there is the existence of the Permanent Five members of the Security Council, whose rivalry has a negative effect on practically all the deliberations and decisions of the council that they judge counter to their national interests.

Possible reforms are listed below, but the list is by no means closed. There is, and always will be, room for new ways to reform a system as massive as the United Nations and for updating practices between now and when those reforms occur.

Before we can embark on a discussion of the question of what to do by way of effective and productive reforms that will lift the United Nations System from the unsatisfactory status quo, there are some basic principles that should be part of the desired reforms.

Crystalizing United Nations Awareness and Culture

The Department of Global Communications at the UN has at its disposal all the ingredients for a modern and updated information system. Yet the messages it tries to convey to its member states about the organization and its work seem not to be reaching their target audiences in member states, whether that be the man in the street, an official in the government, or a businessman. The reason could be intentional, like when national media or commercial media prefer not to favor international United Nations media over more local news. However, member states and their media are part of the United Nations System because their countries are members of that System, and the two media systems should be complementing each other. This could be done by member states continually promoting the United Nations Culture as a concept. A modest example could be to showcase bilateral agreements that states sign among themselves to promote each other's cultures, including their languages, through targeted programming and classroom activities. In the end, it is up to the people in the Department of Public Information at the United Nations to figure out ways to promote the United Nations Culture, but unless this is done tirelessly and with cooperation from national governments, information about the System will remain confined in the United Nations Tower in New York City.

One way to deal with the subject in an effective manner is through symposia organized by the United Nations that can be attended by UN representatives as well as delegates from governments of member states and intellectuals. The recommendations that arise from these symposia should not only be practical but also suitable for a continuous follow-up by representatives from both sides so that with time the concept of a United Nations Culture can sink into the minds of whoever is doing work for the United Nations, be it at the headquarters or in the capitals of various member states. It is very important that this concept of a United Nations Culture be emphasized because it is essential for provoking interest in and dedication to any work connected to or dealing with the United Nations.

Multilateralism vs. Nationalism

The multilateral interests of the United Nations are compatible with the interests of the member states. Despite this, there is an abnormal phenomenon that we witness in the relations between the United Nations and its member states, in that the latter look at and deal with the organization from a national interest standpoint. This approach does not seem compatible with the multilateral approach the UN takes, and when promoting national interests becomes intentional, the results of this attitude become harmful. This conflict explains partly why the UN has lagged in its efforts to change and has struggled to execute its mandate. It should be evident that the two structures, that of the United Nations and the national governments, are distinct and different. One cannot run one system by the methods used by the other. The United Nations policies are drawn up by its principal organs, the General Assembly, the International Security Council, the ECOSOC, and the International Law Court. These policies, when approved, are put into practice by the Secretariat, headed by the secretary-general. When representatives of the United Nations member states participate in the activities of the organization, they should follow the rules of the United Nations and not those of their respective governments. It is a very clear distinction that requires delegates to wear two hats, but not at the same time as the case is right now. Perhaps the source of confusion is that member state delegates draw up the United Nations policies. However, that is not a justification for mixing their roles and thus making the organization work in an unhealthy and unproductive way. Since the establishment of the United Nations in 1945, there has been a hidden fear, especially on the part of certain of its influential member states, that the organization will develop into a world government. Time has since proven that their fear is unfounded simply because no decisions made under the auspices of the United Nations can be passed without the approval of the delegates from member states. Then there is the veto power and the fact that the operation of the United Nations peacekeeping force is fed by observer soldiers who come from member states. Finally, the entire operation is financed by member states. Recently, a rich veto holder disapproved of the way the World Health Organization handled the COVID-19 pandemic and stopped its financial contribution to WHO, putting the organization in a fix since it relies on that country's contribution to operate.

Management vs. Leadership

A question that comes to mind is: Does the organization, in carrying out its work, manage or lead? Before we discuss this question, it is useful to remind ourselves of the differences.

The similarity between management and leadership is that both deal with figuring out what needs to be done, establishing a network of people to do it, and ensuring people do it. But the two approaches differ in the way this is achieved.

Based on these definitions and distinctions, it becomes clear that the present-day United Nations is managing rather than leading when, ideally, the organization should be leading member states in both quantity and quality of work and achievements. Put simply and logically, the whole should lead the parts and not the other way round. For the United Nations, acting as a leader is not in any way wishful thinking. In fact, it is the only way to lift the United Nations from the shadows into the forefront, and to let it show the way

Table 7.1 Management vs. Leadership.

Management	**Leadership**
Management is about orderly and predictable results.	Leadership produces change and is more inductive.
Management is finding the right fit between role and people.	Leadership is the fit between people and vision.
Management is about making it easy for people to complete their job day after day.	Leadership is about touching people at their deepest levels by stirring their sense of belonging, idealism, and self-esteem.

forward in a changing world. However, over the years, the organization has been hijacked by some of its influential member states, who use their financial contributions as leverage to pressure the United Nations into realizing their own national interests. It is not that the United Nations lacks the ability to lead; its hands are tied.

Genuine Reforms

All "reforms" that have occurred over the years seem to be cosmetic. The evidence is there: the veto remains and is exercised; the representative balance between the membership in the International Security Council and the whole membership is not there; the effectiveness of peacekeeping operations leaves a lot to be desired; and developmental projects fail to be realized because of the terms and conditions of borrowing money to execute them. Furthermore, the agency headquarters are located in developed rather than developing countries, and the financial burden that member state contributions to the organization and its subsidiaries place on developing countries weighs increasingly on the shoulders of those states because the size of the budget continually increases.

These are only a few examples of the unsatisfactory status quo that the United Nations finds itself in. Certainly, attempts have been and continue to be made to ameliorate the way things are done, but these attempts are scattered and uncoordinated; if they weren't, the United Nations would have been in better shape after seventy-five years of existence. Given the urgent need for comprehensive, well-prepared, and better-coordinated reforms, the hope is that the United Nations will transform into a good manager, and maybe after a while it will aspire to lead the world. However, it takes two equal partners to achieve that goal, and judging by the present reality, the United Nations and its member states are not in parity. The green light for genuine reforms will come from member states, especially from the influential ones who have veto power. Ideally, the deciding factors of that reform should originate from the whole, not from its parts, but that is the way it is now.

Staff Loyalty in Recruitment and Work

Although staff recruited to work at the United Nations sign a pledge that stipulates allegiance to the organization only, the situation on the ground is far from that. It is human nature that somebody in a position will tend to bring compatriots from their own country to work at headquarters or in the field. It is not uncommon to find a boss and their secretary or assistant coming from the same country. Consequently, the temptation to serve the country through the United Nations is there. We see this too in the United Nations peacekeeping operations, whereby the organization, having no army of its own, has to borrow observer soldiers from its member states. The international civil servant who occupies a position in the Secretariat or the field has a dual responsibility of not recruiting from or favoring assistance to his own country. Being able to separate these components will ensure complete international neutrality and create a healthy environment for productive work. The fact that the United Nations depends on member states for staff, soldiers, and, above all, financial contributions puts it in a compromising position where it can easily be manipulated. It will take hard, patient work to lift the System from this web.

Recommended Actions

Establish a Permanent Multipurpose United Nations Reform Working Group

This Working Group should be charged with reforming the System. It should be permanent and independent but part of the United Nations. Its mandate should cover, in general as well as specifically, the following:

a) Decentralization of decision-making processes and the amalgamation of the agencies.
b) Enlargement of the membership of the International Security Council and the elimination of the veto power.
c) Lessen the financial burden of member states toward the United Nations.
d) Liaise with member states on United Nations affairs.

Decentralize the Decision-making Process of the United Nations Activities and Make the Field the Deciding Factor

This will eliminate duplication, thus saving time and resources. In the same endeavor, regroup the responsibilities of the agencies so that the sole mandate of each agency falls in its area of specialization.

Embark on a Far-reaching Financial Reform That Will Result in a True Decrease in the Burden of Member States

At present, they are in a dire financial situation due to the multiplicity of agencies, programs, and funds that they should contribute to.

Make Decisions Taken by the United Nations General Assembly Binding to the Membership for Application

The General Assembly of any financial institution tells the Board what to do and not the other way round, as is the case in the present relationship between the United Nations General Assembly and its International Security Council.

Enlarge the International Security Council Membership so That a Reasonable Proportion of the General United Nations Membership Is Represented in the Council

At the moment, the ratio is a meager 15 to 193. This is totally undemocratic. The world is dotted with democratic institutions whose parliamentarians preach democracy all the time. There is no reason that their international organization should be spared this privilege and be ruled by autocracy.

Gradual Elimination of the Veto Power

The enlargement of the council should occur in practice right away, and once it is a given, the veto should be eliminated totally. In the meantime, however, the organization could attempt a gradual elimination of the veto power of the Permanent Five. Using the veto to stop any preliminary solution to any problem in the world is an undemocratic exercise that negates logic and thus undermines justice. Originally, the veto power was acquired for a good reason, but that reason no longer exists. However, once the rationale for the veto right disappeared, some holders decided to use it to advance their national interests, a tendency that has had some adverse effect on the work of the United Nations. It is completely logical now to advocate the elimination of that right. Every time the council debates a topic on its agenda in a fair and square manner and presents it in a way becoming of an important international organ like the International Security Council, a veto holder whose country does not approve the ensuing result, and for a national not international reason, can cast a veto on whatever the council decides. Neither the essence of the veto nor its adverse effect on the workings of the council should be tolerated. It is harmful because it prevents the United Nations from functioning in a healthy, productive atmosphere, and it hampers the organization's ability to adapt to changes in the world. The ultimate solution will be an outright elimination of the veto, and if this proves difficult (as expected), then at the very least its use should be restricted—perhaps by limiting the number of vetoes that could be used during each session or by allowing for a veto to be overridden by otherwise unanimous agreement of the full council. Furthermore, casting a veto should be prohibited in life-threatening situations such as a global pandemic or war. Certainly, casting the veto should not be motivated by national interests. Finally, the General Assembly should have a say in overriding the casting of the veto.

Coincidence has it that as we write, another example shows yet again the incapacity of the International Security Council to face problems threatening peace and security in the world—the very heart of its mandate according to Article 24 of the charter. Within the context of the age-old Palestinian Question that started in 1948 when Israel was created on Palestinian land, heavy fighting erupted between the two sides on the eleventh of May 2021, resulting in loss of life and material damage. The fighting started when, as part of Israel's ongoing policy since the occupation, Palestinians were evicted from their homes to make way for Jewish settlements. The first reaction of people around the world was to ask the United Nations to urgently take up the matter so that they could stop the fighting and eventually address this injustice. The International Security Council members convened, but nothing came out of that meeting due to the firm opposition of a veto holder. There was not even a press statement, which is the weakest course of action the council can take in its decision-making process. Due to the intensity of the fighting and the pressure of world public opinion, a second meeting of the council was held, but again to no avail. In the end, a ceasefire was agreed upon between the two parties, but it came about because of the efforts of individual states, not the council. This unsatisfactory and uncomfortable position the council was put in by its own members, especially the veto holders, is a convincing reason to do away with the veto power. The renewed fighting is a fresh and timely reminder of the abnormal situation that the council faces in its work. However, the latest fiasco is only one example in a series of decisions that the council has taken in relation to the Palestinian Question, none of which had any chance of application. This non-application resulted in fighting and wars between the two sides with a considerable loss of life and territories, making it almost impossible to reach a durable and just solution to the enduring question.

Permanency of Council Membership

When the group of nations we now call the Permanent Five acquired veto powers in 1945, it made sense to make their membership permanent, while other members of the council were restricted to terms of two years. It served the interests of these five members and the status quo at the time, but it created an unhealthy working environment for arriving at a productive outcome to any issue. Allowing for the possibility that permanent members can veto or even threaten to veto decisions every time the council considers presenting a draft resolution or simply a declaration on a controversial subject is hardly a convenient atmosphere, let alone productive. The repercussions are felt throughout the System, not just in the workings of the council. Any attempt at reforming any other organ in the United Nations might be subjected to a veto. It is not surprising to see the organization function in an unsatisfactory way. Both the veto and permanent membership adversely affect the ability of the United Nations to do its work, and so the recommendation is to do away with both and give all members of the United Nations an equal chance to present their candidatures for two years.

Increase Proportionally the Ratio Between the Size of the Council and the Size of the General Assembly

This increase will ensure that the council's membership will be truly representative of the organization's membership. Right now, it is not. Member states preach and practice democracy and form relevant institutions for democratic governance in their own countries; they cannot afford to leave the global organization of which they are members to function in an authoritative, unhealthy atmosphere.

Revise Thoroughly the Present System of the United Nations Information Apparatus

Despite a comprehensive information system, there are two major defects. The first lies in the circle of operations handled by the Secretariat, where events concerning the functioning of the United Nations are surrounded by secrecy—an example would be the scandal surrounding the Iraqi Oil-For-Food Programme. This practice of hiding things from the delegates at the General Assembly, the Security Council, and the ECOSOC should be replaced by a system that promotes the free flow of information necessary to clarify things for representatives of member states. The second defect concerns the general public in member states: Citizens of member states should be informed regularly of what the United Nations and the organization are doing, but they are not. There should be a parallel system of information that allows citizens of those countries, members of the United Nations, to remain informed of what is happening at the United Nations.

Embark on a Substantial Financial Reform of the Mother Organization and Its Subsidiaries

The details of how to go about financial reform have been discussed in the book, but the point that should be strongly stressed here is that the ultimate goal should be to reduce and lessen the financial burden that contributions to the budget of all United Nations agencies, funds, and programs place on member states. The dire financial resources of many United Nations members make it impossible for them to pay their dues on a regular basis, and certainly not by the prescribed deadlines. That puts them in arrears all the time. Something must be done urgently to alleviate that burden. Failure to do so will make the situation deteriorate to the point where member states are unable, in part or in whole, to pay their contributions to the United Nations.

To adopt the above-recommended actions and, most importantly, put them into practice, the United Nations has many options available to it. They can form committees, hold seminars, convene meetings, commission experts, or engage in dialogue. However, the goal is always to produce tangible results, results that will ameliorate the actual situation that the United Nations finds itself in and which hampers the work of the organization. The United Nations can form a comprehensive body that will supervise a number of outfits, each taking care of a specific area of reform, be it financial, structural, staff-related, or the grouping of agencies, programs, and funds. The most essential consideration is to get away from making cosmetic changes and to start making genuine, substantial reforms that will lead to real changes.

Note on Sounding the Alarm

The United Nations at a Crossroads

The challenge addressed by this book, namely adapting the United Nations to a changing world, remains unresolved, and there is a risk that it will be that way for some time to come. This book and other literature about the United Nations roam around the same searching questions: What can the United Nations do, and what can it not do? Where has it succeeded and where has it failed? In the case of failure, can it be reformed or not? And finally, where do we go from here? These are basically the same questions Karen Mingst, Margaret Karns, and Alynna Lyons ask in their book, *The United Nations in the 21st Century*. They quote former deputy secretary-general and administrator of UNDP Mark Malloch Brown, who says, "The intergovernmental gridlock between the big contributors and the rest of the membership concerning governance and voting is the core of dysfunction" and "Until the sense of crisis of the United Nations is strong enough to make governments let go of their own agendas, there cannot be the kind of cathartic recommitment and renewal of the United Nations proper that is required."[1] In other words, and we have said the same in this book, unless member states forego their national interests in managing United Nations affairs, the organization cannot operate in a productive way. Such sacrifice, i.e., prioritizing international interests over national ones, is imperative for a better United Nations. Immediately, a practical question comes to mind: Is this possible? The immediate answer, judging by what we witness in world politics today and have seen for a long time, is that this is almost impossible.

The remote possibility of seeing nations put international interests ahead of their own can be found in the attitude of the big veto-holding five, who will stand in the way of such progress. An example might demonstrate that. At the start of every month during my time on the Security Council, members received an agenda, and each got a turn to comment on every item. When the turn of one of the heads of delegations that belong to the P5 category came, he started to comment on the agenda items following the script his delegation had prepared for him. Halfway through, he got tired and turned to one of his diplomats, saying, "Do I have to do all this for the whole world?" meaning the topics covering the whole world. One would assume that since he was in the International Security Council, the answer would be yes. His diplomat answered him, "We are the world." Suffice to say that the answer reflects the thinking of the P5 members, or at least some of them. They not only do not distinguish between international issues and national interests, but they also make the former part of the latter and act accordingly.

Should the almost unattainable objective of reform deter us from trying? No, those of us who support the United Nations and believe in its goals should make the challenge a source of stubborn determination in our continuous attempts at reforming the System. It makes it more urgent and necessary. Hence, Sounding the Alarm.

Since the exercise of reforming the United Nations is complicated and multifaceted, owing to the size of the organization, it will take time. What is most important is to always keep the dialogue about reform alive by engaging in continuous gatherings at which these matters can be raised, i.e., organize meetings, initiate discussions, and suggest recommendations. What we need to avoid is creating a system in which meetings and conferences succeed each other in a vicious circle. That will only serve those who want to avoid reforms through delaying tactics. Meetings and conferences for reforms should go hand in hand with a continuous dialogue among all concerned, especially the decision-makers.

It is true that reforming the United Nations Security Council is important and should be the ultimate focus of reform, but there are areas outside the council and inside the United Nations that also need reform. Take the Secretariat, for example. It has succeeded in avoiding the reform spotlight. One must remember that although member states contribute the money for the United Nations budget, it is the Secretariat that controls the spending.

Thus, instances of the disappearance or misuse of funds, whether intentional or not, can be avoided. Furthermore, the last months of every year witness a rush to spend that year's appropriations to make way for next year's new budget, which increases the likelihood that mistakes might be made.

When it comes to reform, we also need to consider the ways and methods by which the Secretariat prepares the material for executing various approved programs. It bombards member states with related documentation that is so intricate that some member states with limited means and staff at their disposal cannot cope with the volume of material or the complexity of the content, let alone apply what is required. This inability to grasp material and apply the recommendations repeats itself on a yearly basis. To rectify this situation, it might be necessary for the United Nations to initiate training programs for those personnel and officials whose work is related to the organization. The training should concentrate on how and why the United Nations is functioning. After all, member states have the right to know how and why their contribution money is spent.

Related to the above, the General Assembly and the Security Council discovered purely by accident during the Oil-for-Food scandal that there is a cloud of secrecy within the Secretariat. Both organs were so taken by surprise that Secretary-General Kofi Annan saw the necessity of opening up the workings of the Secretariat. It is not known how much of that was achieved and whether the phenomenon was thoroughly investigated. However, the size of the Secretariat and the huge task it is entrusted with both certainly merit reform. We can draw hope from the fact that the current secretary-general, António Guterres, is as enthusiastic about reform as his predecessor, Kofi Annan.

Reforming the Security Council will be the most difficult part to achieve. Permanent membership, the veto, and the fact that the council's decisions are binding on the entire membership of the United Nations all stand in the way of reform. And yet despite this, the council has taken positive decisions by approving the following:

- In 1965, Article 23 of the United Nations Charter was amended to enlarge the Security Council membership from 11 to 15 members.

- In 1965, Article 27 was amended to increase the required number of Security Council votes from 7 to 9.
- In 1965, Article 61 was amended to enlarge the Economic and Social membership from 18 to 27.
- In 1968, Article 109 was amended to change the requirements for a General Conference of Member States for reviewing the charter.
- In 1973, Article 61 was amended again to further enlarge the Economic and Social membership from 27 to 54.

Those amendments were passed, which tells us that in the past, the Permanent Five have been willing to listen and cooperate to the benefit of the organization and not only act to the benefit of their own national interests. The question that comes to mind is why this cooperation stopped after the sixties and the seventies. A few searching questions could help determine why this change of heart occurred. What is it they want and do not have? Would they be willing to override the veto and replace it with a majority of fourteen votes? Would they agree to limiting the number of times they could use the veto on a single issue? Would they agree to limit the number of vetoes they are allowed per session? This list of questions is by no means comprehensive, but exploring the questions and discovering the answers might lead to further reforms that will end the partial paralysis that currently hampers the work of the organization and prevents modifications that reflect the changes in the world.

Casting the veto is a sign of weakness, not strength, and it is sustained by the power of the purse or by military might. It is an assault on the human mind's ability to find an equitable solution to a problem. Casting a veto is like using weapons in a discussion room instead of on the battlefield. This is a flagrant contradiction of the founding principle stipulated in the United Nations Charter, which mandates the organization to make peace, not war.

In 2020, on the occasion of the organization's seventy-fifth birthday, *The Economist* dedicated a ten-page inner supplement in one of its issues to the United Nations. The cover of that supplement showed a tilted mast bearing the United Nations flag and bore the banner "UNhappy birthday." The information inside, as well as the analysis, was concise and to the point, detailing the ills presently faced by the organization and showing how these concerns lie at the heart of the organization's unsatisfactory role in world affairs. Even the headings are indicative of that role: Missing in action. Who's in charge? Mission impossible. Grand redesigns.

In sounding the alarm for a fresh look at the United Nations, it may be worth engaging the serious press; it would be even better if the press felt the need to look at reform at the UN, just as *The Economist* did. The press can reach the broader public more than scattered books dealing with parts of the subject can. We pray that such a broader readership will include people who take decisions concerning the United Nations and that the subject of a fresh look at the organization includes genuine reforms.

Ultimately, it is not possible for decision-makers to go into the details of reforming the United Nations if, to begin with, they do not have the intention and the will to undertake those reforms. Merely convincing them that reform is necessary will fall short if believing in reforms does not sink into their minds. It will take a lot of intellectual, conceptual, and political effort to do that, especially since those decision-makers continue to make decisions that favor the national interests of their governments rather than those of international organizations like the United Nations, which requires a multilateral approach.

The ills that the United Nations suffers from and the suggested remedies have been treated here as well as in special reports and books, and by the supplement in *The Economist*, other magazines, and newspapers. So why sound the alarm? Simply because the ills are still there and have been for seventy-five years. Suggested reforms always fall short for two fundamental reasons. The first is that an international issue cannot be considered on the same footing as a national one. We cannot handle national issues in the same way we handle international ones. The United Nations is not a government ministry; neither the terms of reference nor the actions are the same. Therefore, it is not possible to deal with the United Nations in the same way as you run a ministry. However, this is what is happening and has happened all along under the pretext of sovereignty. If one treats the United Nations affairs from a nationalist standpoint, one is supposing that the national interests of member states are the same, or at least complementary. Alas, this is not what we see in our world today. On the contrary, national interests often contradict each other, and this leads to clashes when discussing international matters. These conflicts of interest reflect negatively on dealing with the United Nations and have caused the unsatisfactory situation that the organization finds itself in.

The second reason why efforts at reform fail has often been stated: the existence of the veto power. It is unthinkable that anyone who holds the veto power will use it to object to any issue that is beneficial to the United Nations because that will be against the international principles spelled out in the charter. Yet what we witness, and have witnessed before, is that the veto is cast in response to issues that the holder's government considers against the country's national interests. This is a phenomenon that should not be seen in the international context of the United Nations, as it causes confusion when representatives try to deal with national interests in an international setting.

Diplomats accredited to the United Nations and officials working in the organization are very much aware that these discrepancies are the main element contributing to the unsatisfactory functioning of the United Nations. International Security Council delegates are very interested in the lively debate surrounding increasing membership to the council, whether temporary or permanent, because according to the co-chair of the intergovernmental group set up for this purpose, because this issue speaks to their core national interests. This is hardly what is needed to rehabilitate the United Nations. What is desired is a focus on this issue as an international one rather than a national one, so that it fits the United Nations mandate. The current secretary-general of the organization, António Guterres, clearly understands this when he says in effect, today we have a multilateralism that has no teeth, and whenever there are teeth, as in the Security Council, there is no appetite to bite. Both quotations presented here are very telling regarding the unhappy birthday, and they clearly point to the attitude of the United Nations member states in prioritizing their national interests when it comes to dealing with the United Nations issues. In the absence of strong teeth and a big appetite, sounding the alarm is the only option.

Ideally, the United Nations should have its own fund from which it can finance its budget and that of its subsidiaries. It is up to its accountants to figure out the best way to establish that independent fund. But this we can be assured of: independent funding will spare the organization the agony of member states being constantly in arrears. At the same time, the United Nations should have its own army, one that is not borrowed from member states but that is recruited from these states. Having its own permanent force will facilitate its ability to deal with international crises. Securing the independence of the United Nations in these two areas is not unlike the supposed neutrality of its staff. However, this call for independence is logical and necessary, but almost impossible to realize, given the unsatisfactory and unhealthy state of the United Nations at present. By securing change in those two areas, the organization will acquire an independent power in its decision-making process.

Throughout this book, we have in fact sounded the alarm, considering various details, appealing to those who have access to decision-making regarding the United Nations' functions and operations to listen. Unfortunately, the biggest challenge is that these people lack information about the organization, either because they haven't got enough zeal for United Nations affairs or they are too busy attending to their own national preoccupations. The advantages the Permanent Five have at present do not make them enthusiastic to change the way the organization works and to make it function better. By the same token, one should not entirely disregard the Secretariat, which constitutes a world of its own. For the most part, the Secretariat appears to be happy with things as they are, or they have given up on reforming the organization because of the negative attitude among those members who have the deciding say in the matter.

Had things in the United Nations, its main organs, and subsidiaries looked better, or if they had at least started to follow the required path of recovery, "Sounding the Alarm" would have been a chapter focused on what remains to be done in terms of reform at the United Nations. However, we are not even at the beginning of the stages where we think that the United Nations has reached the level of an effective, productive organization. The whole book, therefore, constitutes an alarm, and the last chapter is a reminder that we have a moral and material responsibility as members of the United Nations to make it function in a better way. No matter what we achieve by way of development in our own countries, these efforts will not be complete if we do not reform the organization to which we belong.

Whatever has been done by way of reform thus far is unsatisfactory by any standard. We desire much more for the international organization that we have entrusted with peace and development in the world that we live in. There is no better and clearer example to illustrate this than the fierce competitions and conflicts that we witness in our world at present, at the expense of cooperation and intent among member states of the United Nations. If we reform the United Nations to make it function better, we will certainly see a more harmonious world than the one we inhabit today. The job of reform has started in the most timid way imaginable, but is far from being accomplished.

Reforming an organization is a serious business, and when it involves an organization as vast as the United Nations, the task is daunting. It is not a matter of an officer thinking that if he does his job in this way instead of that way, that this will amount to reform. We are dealing here with an outfit that has whole countries, countries of varying sizes, resources, and potential, as members. Many of these countries themselves need reforming. The United Nations, in principle at least, is mandated to manage its affairs as far as peace and development are concerned. One should also remember that operating the United Nations is not similar to the way member states operate individually. Confusing the way these systems work makes the United Nations less effective.

The end of this book is not the end of the story of reforming the United Nations. Rather, it is the beginning. Real reforming requires more than what has occurred to date, and only real and meaningful change in the way the United Nations operates will allow it to cope with a changing world.

Note

1 Karen A. Mingst, Margaret P. Karns, and Alynna J. Lyon, *The United Nations in the 21st Century*. New York: Routledge, 2019, n.pag.

Bibliography

"Key Data on UNESCO Staff." Management Support and Coordination Unit (HRM/MSC), January 2022, rev. April 6, 2022. https://en.unesco.org/sites/default/files/key_data_jan_2022_0.pdf.

"UN Trusteeship Council Documentation." Dag Hammarskjöld Library. https://research.un.org/en/docs/tc/territories.

"UNhappy Birthday on the UN 75th Anniversary." The Economist Special Report, June 20–26, 2020.

"The UN's Structures Built in 1945 Are Not Fit for 2020, Let Alone Beyond It." Special Report. The Economist, June 18, 2020. https://www.economist.com/special-report/2020/06/18/the-uns-structures-built-in-1945-are-not-fit-for-2020-let-alone-beyond-it.

Banbury, Anthony. "I Love the U.N., but It Is Failing." New York Times, March 18, 2016. https://www.nytimes.com/2016/03/20/opinion/sunday/i-love-the-un-but-it-is-failing.html.

Bosco, David. "When the Blue Helmets Are to Blame." Foreign Policy, July 22, 2014. https://foreignpolicy.com/2014/07/22/when-the-blue-helmets-are-to-blame/.

Buallay, Jassim. Bahrain in the International Security Council: 1998-1999. In Arabic. Ministry of Information, 2006.

International Court of Justice. Charter of the United Nations. https://www.icj-cij.org/charter-of-the-united-nations.

International Court of Justice. Statute of the International Court of Justice. https://www.icj-cij.org/charter-of-the-united-nations.

Kant, Emmanuel. *Perpetual Peace: A Philosophical Essay*. Translated by Campbell Smith. London: Swan Sonnenschein, 1903 [1795].

Mingst, Karen A., Margaret P. Karns, and Alynna J. Lyon. *The United Nations in the 21st Century*. New York: Routledge, 2019.

Mires, Charlene. *Capital of the World: The Race to Host the United Nations*. 5th ed. New York: NYU Press, 2019.

Muravchik, Joshua. *The Future of the United Nations: Understanding the Past to Chart a Way Forward*. Washington, DC: AEI Press, 2005.

Otterman, Sharon. "What Is the Controversy over the UN Oil-for-Food Program?" Backgrounder prepared for the Council on Foreign Relations, October 28, 2005. https://www.cfr.org/backgrounder/iraq-oil-food-scandal.

Popovski, Vesselin. "Reforming and Innovating the United Nations Security Council." Background paper prepared for the Commission on Global Security Justice & Governance. The Hague Institute for Global Justice, 2015. https://www.stimson.org/wp-content/files/Commission_BP_Popovski1.pdf.

The South Centre Analytical Note. *Meeting the Challenges of UN Reform: A South Perspective.* Geneva: The South Centre, August 2006. https://www.southcentre.int/wp-content/uploads/2013/07/AN_GPG1_UN-Reform-South-Perspective_EN.pdf.

United Nations Peacebuilding Commission. *A More Secure World: Our Shared Responsibility. Report of the High-level Panel on Threats, Challenges and Change.* New York: UN, 2004.

van Kappen, Franklin. "Report Dated 1 May 1996 of the Secretary-General's Military Adviser Concerning the Shelling of the United Nations Compound at Qana on April 18, 1996." An annex to a letter from the secretary-general addressed to the president of the Security Council, May 7, 1996. https://www.un.org/unispal/document/auto-insert-187312/.

Index

About the Author

His Excellency Ambassador Jassim Mohammed Buallay is a retired Bahraini diplomat and international civil servant. From 1970 to 1974, Ambassador Buallay served at the United Nations Educational, Scientific and Cultural Organization (UNESCO) in Paris. Subsequently, he was appointed as the Kingdom of Bahrain's first ambassador to France (1974 to 1979), vice chair of the United Nations Children's Fund (UNICEF) Executive Board (1984 to 1985), and ambassador to Tunisia, Morocco, and Algeria (1987 to 1994). In 1994, he became the permanent representative of Bahrain to the United Nations in New York City. During his tenure at the United Nations, Bahrain was elected to the United Nations Security Council.

Ambassador Buallay served as president of that august body in December 1998, during which the Security Council met to address the Balkans crisis, specifically the conflict between Serbs and Albanians. Immediately after that, he secured Bahrain's membership in the UN Economic and Social Council (ECOSOC). He served as vice-president of ECOSOC in 2002, which provided him with insights into how the United Nations undertakes its economic and social agenda.

Since retiring from diplomatic service in 2006, Ambassador Buallay has continued to write and speak about global affairs, particularly the effectiveness of the UN in promoting and realizing international peace in the world. He also teaches and lectures at higher education institutions around the world with the purpose of passing on his experience for the benefit of the new generation. He is the author of *Bahrain in the International Security Council: 1998–99* (2006), a monograph that reflects his experience in global security and peacekeeping.

Ambassador Buallay earned his bachelor's degree from the American University of Beirut and obtained his Master of Science in International Organizations from Long Island University's Brooklyn Campus. He is the recipient of numerous awards and recognitions, including France's ordre national du Mérite (with grade of Knight), the Moroccan Order of Ouissam Allawite (First Grade), the Republic of Tunisia National Order of Merit (First Grade), and the Kingdom of Bahrain Order of Sheikh Isa bin Salman Al Khalifa (Third Class).

www.ingramcontent.com/pod-product-compliance
Ingram Content Group UK Ltd.
Pitfield, Milton Keynes, MK11 3LW, UK
UKHW020208290926
15470UKWH00001B/61

9 781683 933878